Building Bridges Across the Racial Divide

This book is part of the Peter Lang Education list.
Every volume is peer reviewed and meets
the highest quality standards for content and production.

PETER LANG
New York • Bern • Berlin
Brussels • Vienna • Oxford • Warsaw

Larry Feldman and Sandy Feldman

Building Bridges Across the Racial Divide

PETER LANG
New York • Bern • Berlin
Brussels • Vienna • Oxford • Warsaw

Library of Congress Cataloging-in-Publication Data

Names: Feldman, Larry, author. | Feldman, Sandy, author.
Title: Building bridges across the racial divide / Larry Feldman and Sandy Feldman.
Description: New York: Peter Lang, 2019.
Includes bibliographical references and index.
Identifiers: LCCN 2018058156 | ISBN 978-1-4331-6070-7 (hardback: alk. paper)
ISBN 978-1-4331-7296-0 (paperback: alk. paper) | ISBN 978-1-4331-6034-9 (ebook pdf)
ISBN 978-1-4331-6035-6 (epub) | ISBN 978-1-4331-6036-3 (mobi)
Subjects: LCSH: United States—Race relations—Study and teaching.
Anti-racism—Study and teaching—United States.
Racism—Study and teaching—United States.
Classification: LCC E185.615.F3955 2019 | DDC 305.800973—dc23
LC record available at https://lccn.loc.gov/2018058156
DOI 10.3726/b15198

Bibliographic information published by **Die Deutsche Nationalbibliothek.**
Die Deutsche Nationalbibliothek lists this publication in the "Deutsche
Nationalbibliografie"; detailed bibliographic data are available
on the Internet at http://dnb.d-nb.de/.

The paper in this book meets the guidelines for permanence and durability
of the Committee on Production Guidelines for Book Longevity
of the Council of Library Resources.

To Our Sons
Jeremy, Liam, Ben and Jonah
Our Daughters-In-Law
Jessica and Greta
Our Grandchildren
Jackson, Isaac and Emilia
and
To All Who Have Joined Us in Building Bridges Across the Racial Divide

Table of Contents

Preface

More than fifty years after passage of the Civil Rights Act, Americans from different racial groups continue to live in largely segregated worlds. With limited exceptions we reside in different neighborhoods, socialize in different settings, and pray in different houses of worship. Our children continue to attend schools that are, for the most part, as racially segregated as they were at the time of the Civil Rights movement. Our perceptions of one another are often distorted by generations of separation, alienation and mistrust. Our reactions to one another are negatively affected by stereotypes, prejudice, anger, and fear. In the words of Dr. Martin Luther King, Jr.: "We fear each other because we don't know each other; we don't know each other because we are so often separated from each other." (King, 1958).

Dr. King dreamed of a world in which everyone would be judged by the content of their character rather than the color of their skin. If such a world is ever going to exist it is critically important to find ways to bridge the racial divide. Children and adolescents, the architects of the future, need to be empowered to reach across artificial barriers and build relationships based on mutual understanding, respect, and trust. Adults need to provide role models for the next generation.

In this book we present principles and practices for helping children, teenagers, and adults take steps to begin to know one another in authentic ways, learn about each other's individual interests and abilities, reduce the power of stereotypes and prejudice, and establish a true sense of community. We illustrate these principles and practices with examples drawn from our own experience with a variety of diversity initiatives, and from an extensive review of research on effective diversity initiatives in communities and in schools.

In our work as diversity consultants; individual, group and family therapists; and college instructors teaching a course on *The Psychology of Stereotypes and Prejudice*, we are often struck by the powerful impact societal and familial belief systems can have on the feelings, thoughts, and behaviors of children and adults. We all absorb attitudes communicated (consciously or unconsciously; directly or indirectly) by family members, friends, neighbors, teachers, clergy, and the media. Once established, these attitudes prompt behaviors (separation, wariness, hostility, etc.) that reinforce stereotypes and perpetuate mistrust and fear. We often see what we anticipate seeing; we often view "the other" through a distorted lens.

Overcoming these barriers requires on-going, positive contact over time. In *Building Bridges across the Racial Divide*, we present guidelines for structuring, maintaining, and reinforcing such contact.

Our own racial/ethnic identities are European-American and Jewish. The "white" skin that comes from our European heritage helps us to understand the perspective of the dominant majority group. Our Jewish identity helps us to understand the perspective of discriminated-against minorities. We know that we can never fully comprehend the unique experience of any other individual or group, but we believe that our "majority and minority" status has been helpful in our efforts to empathize with members of different groups and to serve as facilitators in various types of diversity initiatives.

Congressman John Lewis, in his book about the history of the Civil Rights movement, shares an old African proverb: "When you pray, move your feet." He goes on to say: "As a nation, if we care for the Beloved Community, we must move our feet, our hands, our hearts, our resources to build and not to tear down, to reconcile and not to divide, to love and not to hate, to heal and not to kill. In the final analysis, we are one people, one family, one house—the American house, the American family" (Lewis, 1998). It is our hope that *Building Bridges Across the Racial Divide* can help all of us "move our feet" a little closer to this ideal.

References

King, M. L. (1958). Advice for living. *Ebony, 13*(7), 112.

Lewis, J. with D'Orso, M. (1998). *Walking with the wind: A memoir of the movement.* New York, NY: Simon & Schuster.

Acknowledgments

We have been privileged to work with many wonderful people on the diversity initiatives we describe in this book. Our friends in Project Unity, the Race Relations Council, the All God's Children Community Choir, Calling All Colors, Healing Racism, and the Council for World Class communities have enriched our lives in a multitude of ways. Not only have their talents and commitment contributed significantly to the success of these initiatives, but their friendships have greatly enhanced the quality of our lives. We have learned and grown from our interactions with the students in our college class and in Calling All Colors and from the children, teens, and families of the All God's Children Choir.

We appreciate the help of many friends and family members who read earlier versions of one or more chapters of the book and gave us helpful suggestions. Most recently we have benefitted from the support and valuable feedback offered by Michael Nixon, Vice President of Diversity and Inclusion at Andrews University.

Our editors at Peter Lang—Sarah Bode, Megan Madden, Monica Baum, and Janell Harris, have been helpful every step of the way.

Chapter 1

Why Is Diversity Important?

The United States is rapidly becoming an extremely diverse country. In the most recent census, more than half of the children under one year of age were from racial minority groups (United States Census Bureau, 2012). As these children grow up, they are likely to encounter a society that has no racial majority.

Work environments are becoming increasingly diverse. In order to be successful in such environments, confidence in one's ability to work with individuals from a variety of racial/ethnic backgrounds is essential. In a legal brief regarding an affirmative action case being heard by the U.S. Supreme Court (Fischer v University of Texas, 2015), forty-five major corporations argued that a talent pool that includes people with experience working in racially diverse groups is essential to their continued success. These corporations insisted that without the ability to work comfortably and competently in a racially diverse environment, their employees and management will be ill-equipped to compete in an increasingly diverse world. In the same case, a similar brief was filed by a group of former high-ranking military and civilian leaders of the U.S. armed forces. These officials reviewed the severe problems that racial segregation had previously created for military units and the important contribution that racial diversity has made to military efficiency and productivity. Like the business leaders, military leaders emphasized the significance of diverse learning experiences in helping young people develop confidence in their ability to work in diverse environments.

In order to create a well-functioning diverse environment, the barriers initiated and maintained by racial segregation—stereotypes, prejudice, and discrimination—must be confronted. What are the characteristics of these barriers?

Stereotypes, Prejudice, and Discrimination

Stereotypes are "overgeneralized" beliefs—they paint every member of a group with the same brush. These beliefs are sometimes positive (for example, "African-Americans are great basketball players"; "Asian-Americans excel in math and science") but they are much more often negative (for example, "African-Americans are lazy"; "Asian-Americans are humorless"). Whether positive or negative, stereotypes interfere with accurate perception because they substitute a generalization for the actual characteristics of a particular individual.

Stereotypes lead to *prejudice*—positive or negative attitudes and feelings toward members of a particular group. Positive prejudice (prejudice in favor of a group) is usually reserved for members of one's own group (for example, a White person who has the attitude: "I always trust White people"; a Black person who has the attitude: "I always trust Black people"). Negative prejudice (prejudice against a group) is usually generated toward members of "other" groups (for example, a White person who has the attitude "I don't trust Black people"; a Black person who has the attitude: "I don't trust White people").

Prejudicial attitudes generate *discriminatory behavior*. Discrimination tips the scales in favor of a particular group (most often one's own group) and against one or more "other" groups. For example, a White employer who favors White employees when it comes time for promotions ("I know they'll be responsible and reliable"), and refuses to promote Black employees because he views them as "irresponsible and unreliable."

Intergroup Contact Theory

How can stereotypes, prejudice, and discrimination be prevented or diminished? In 1954, psychologist Gordon Allport provided ground-breaking answers to these questions with his Intergroup Contact Theory (Allport, 1954). Allport suggested that contact between members of different racial and ethnic groups was the most effective means for reducing negative attitudes and beliefs. But not just any contact would do. Allport postulated that four conditions—personal acquaintance, equal status, shared goals and cooperative interactions, and support by relevant authorities—are needed in order for contact to have these desired effects.

Personal Acquaintance

Personal acquaintance involves getting to know someone, rather than just sharing the same space. If contact is to lead to significant change in attitudes and behavior, people need to form personal connections with one another. Genuine interactions—conversations, shared activities, etc.—are an integral part of the change process. Individuals from different groups need to have opportunities to spend time together, to recognize each other by name, to talk about their interests, to share their thoughts, feelings, and life experiences. Merely being in the same space, without personal interaction, is not likely to produce significant positive change.

Equal Status

The condition of equal status refers to treating members of all groups as equals. Intergroup contact is most likely to be effective when all participants have equal status within the contact situation. If there is equal status, everyone has the same opportunity to participate in the activities of the group and no one has control over anyone else (adults, of course, do have control over children but this control must be carefully and consistently applied, and done so without regard to race). Contact in which there is a status hierarchy—for example, a mixed-race choir in which soloists are drawn from only one racial group—is not likely to lead to positive change. Equal status within the group is essential in order to counter the effects of unequal status, based on stereotypes and prejudice, within the larger society. Equal status communicates clearly that all participants bring value to the experience, that all participants are worth knowing, and that everyone benefits from each person's contribution.

Shared Goals and Cooperative Interactions

This condition involves working together toward a common objective. Allport suggests that: "Only the type of contact that leads people to *do* things together is likely to result in changed attitudes (...) Common participation and common interests are more effective than the bare fact of equal-status contact." (Allport, 1954, p. 276). He illustrates this principle with the example of multi-ethnic athletic teams: "Here the goal is all-important; the ethnic composition of the team is irrelevant. It is the cooperative striving for the goal that engenders solidarity" (Allport, 1954, p. 276).

Working together toward a common goal leads to a sense of interdependence, of each person needing the other (or others) to achieve the shared objective. Such interdependence promotes recognition of the others' strengths, the specific value added by their participation, and therefore is a powerful force for reducing stereotypes and prejudice. As individuals come to know each other, their picture of "what those people are like" begins to change, to become more complex, to become more real.

Cooperative interaction is an important condition for prejudice-reducing contact. Competitive interaction, on the other hand, is not. Extending Allport's example, two racially segregated teams competing against one another is not a formula for reducing stereotypes and prejudice. Indeed, it is more likely a formula for reinforcing these distorted attitudes and beliefs. In the heat of competition, players may project (consciously or unconsciously) a stereotypic caricature of "the other" onto their opponents, and then respond to the stereotype rather than the actual person with whom they are competing.

Support by Relevant Authorities

Change-promoting contact requires sanction and support by relevant authorities: parents, clergy, teachers, school administrators, government officials, etc. In addition to providing official sanction for the contact, community leaders can be very helpful in connecting individuals and families, recruiting participants, and facilitating program development.

Without the support of relevant authorities, contact is unlikely to lead to positive change. For example, racial integration of schools without the support of teachers and administrators is not likely to lead to a reduction of racial stereotypes and prejudice. Such contact may actually increase those attitudes and beliefs.

One Additional Condition

Based on our work with a variety of diversity initiatives, we have added one more condition for effective contact: *Modeling by Adult Leaders*. Talking about diversity is not enough; adults need to demonstrate that people from different racial backgrounds can come together in an atmosphere of equality and mutual respect. This principle is especially important when children are involved—adult leaders need to "walk the walk" as well as "talk the talk."

Reducing Stereotypes and Prejudice

Allport's ideas have stood the test of time. A comprehensive review of hundreds of research studies of his Intergroup Contact Theory (Pettigrew & Tropp, 2006) found clear and compelling evidence that positive contact between members of different groups reduces stereotypes and prejudice. When the contact experience was most clearly and systematically structured in accordance with Allport's conditions, the strongest reduction in prejudice occurred. Experiences that contained all of the conditions were ideal, but even when only some of the conditions were met, positive effects were produced.

Intergroup friendship has been identified as a particularly powerful means for producing positive change. When friendship crosses racial and ethnic lines, stereotypes and prejudice are dramatically reduced (Davies, Tropp, Aron, Pettigrew, & Wright, 2011; Pettigrew & Tropp, 2006).

Some studies (Harwood, 2016) have found that musical collaborations are a particularly effective arena for the development of intergroup friendships. There is evidence that such collaborations have direct positive effects on the participants and indirect positive effects on those who observe and listen.

What are the effects of positive interracial contact on children and adolescents? Many studies have examined this question. One clear finding is that elementary and middle school students who have greater amounts of such contact develop more tolerant and inclusive viewpoints about individuals from different racial groups (Killen, Crystal, & Ruck, 2007). Greater levels of contact are associated with lower levels of prejudice, and when optimal conditions for intergroup contact are established larger reductions occur (Amicus brief, 2006). Also, students who have greater levels of intergroup contact are more likely to evaluate exclusion of individuals on the basis of group membership as wrong and harmful. For example, in one study a young student's reaction to the idea of such exclusion was: "It's not fair to use race as a reason not to be friends with someone; it's kind of like being prejudiced" (Killen et al., 2007, p. 70).

Similar results are found in research with college students. Having the opportunity to socialize with individuals from a different racial group and to discuss racial issues enhances students' level of cultural awareness and their commitment to promoting racial understanding (Chang, Astin, & Kim, 2004). As campus diversity increases, the likelihood of cross-racial friendships increases. The development of such friendships is associated with a significant decrease in stereotypes and prejudice and a significant increase in mutual understanding and trust (Fischer, 2008).

Some studies have demonstrated that merely observing positive intergroup contact can stimulate a reduction in stereotypes and prejudice. Psychologist Stephen Wright and his associates (Wright, Aron, McLaughlin-Volpe, & Ropp, 1997) found that when individuals observe someone from their own racial group being friends with someone from a different racial group, the observers themselves demonstrate less prejudice toward the other group. Further, the more individuals the person knows from his or her own group who have friends in the other group, the lower their prejudice score. A study by another group of researchers (Schiappa, Gregg & Hewes, 2006) demonstrated that watching television shows that portray positive intergroup contact is associated with lower levels of prejudice. A third study (Miles & Crisp, 2014) found that imagined contact—visualizing an intergroup interaction—was helpful in changing perceptions of social norms and reducing anxiety about engaging in such contact. The findings from these studies demonstrate the benefits that positive intergroup contact can bring to those who just observe or visualize, but do not directly participate in, these interactions.

Increased Comfort Interacting with Racially Diverse Individuals

Segregation frequently leads to discomfort interacting with people from racial groups different from one's own. Lack of contact, combined with negative stereotypes, promotes mistrust and fear. Mistrust and fear create further discomfort, distance, misinterpretations, and alienation. It is difficult to be "at ease" if you are operating on false information or no real information at all. Caricatures thrive in the absence of authentic interactions.

A number of researchers have studied the effects of positive interracial contact on individuals' comfort level interacting with those of a different race. It's helpful to look closely at the experiences of students in successfully integrated schools to examine the impact of diversity on relationships with individuals different than oneself. One study found that students of all racial/ethnic groups who attend more diverse schools have higher comfort levels with members of racial groups different than their own (Kurlaender & Yun, 2007). In another study, White students in integrated settings exhibited more racial tolerance and less fear of their Black peers than their counterparts in segregated environments (Schofield, 1995). In a racially diverse high school in Cambridge, Massachusetts, researchers found that substantial majorities of students report a strong level of comfort with members of other racial and ethnic groups and that their school experiences increased their level of understanding of diverse points of view. (Civil Rights Project, 2002). The students in this study were asked to write about their personal views on the question of what they "learned or gained from attending school with people who are of a racial or ethnic group different from your own?" One student, who had transferred into public school, wrote: "I came from an all-white private school. CRLS [Cambridge High School] has conquered many fears that I had about people from different racial and ethnic groups. I feel very thankful." Diversity was seen as responsible for expanding the world view of another: "I have been exposed to more cultures and greater diversity than I ever could have imagined. I value my experience in public school much more because of this." A third student noted how diversity in the high school not only helped his understanding of others but also prompted him to think about his own background: "I have not only grown very comfortable with people from different racial or ethnic groups, but I have come to be excited and interested by such difference. I have learned to respect others while still being true to my own heritage and beliefs." These examples highlight the growth-enhancing opportunities provided by diverse learning environments.

Increased Confidence Working in Racially Diverse Settings

Research further supports the idea that positive interracial contact promotes the development of cross-cultural competence, an essential skill for working in racially diverse settings. In three different studies, graduates of racially integrated high schools were interviewed about the impact of their school experiences on their performance at work

(Eaton, 2001; Wells & Frankenberg, 2007; Wells, Duran, & White, 2008). One of these studies summarizes the results in these words:

> Preparation for working in a diverse setting—the "diversity rationale"—was, for these graduates, by far the most obvious and pragmatic outcome of their experiences in desegregated public schools. The vast majority of graduates we interviewed said that at work in particular, they draw on the skills they learned in their desegregated public schools, skills of getting along and feeling comfortable with people of divergent backgrounds and cultures. (Wells et al., 2008, p. 2532)

A large-scale study investigated the effects of racial diversity in medical school (Saha, Guiton, Wimmers, & Wilkerson, 2008). The responses of more than 20,000 graduating students from more than 100 medical schools were examined, and students from more racially diverse schools were compared with those from less diverse schools. The researchers found that White students who attend racially diverse medical schools felt better prepared than students at less diverse schools to care for patients from racial or ethnic groups other than their own. They also found that in order to achieve the full educational benefits of diversity, medical schools needed to actively promote positive interaction among students from different backgrounds. The authors argued that because of the significance of the doctor/patient relationship in the provision of quality health care, it is critical that medical schools take these findings, and all their possible ramifications, seriously.

Increased Comfort Living in Racially Diverse Neighborhoods

We know that racial segregation tends to perpetuate itself over the life cycle. Growing up in a segregated neighborhood and attending predominantly segregated schools greatly increases the likelihood of living in a segregated neighborhood as an adult. Might positive interracial contact interrupt this cycle? Studies of diversity on college campuses (Gurin, 1999a) strongly suggest the answer is yes. Students who attend racially diverse colleges and universities are much more likely than those who attend more racially homogeneous institutions to live and work after graduation in more racially diverse settings. They are also more likely to have a racially diverse network of friends. Researcher Patricia Gurin believes that these findings have important implications: "If institutions of higher education are able to bring together students from various ethnic and racial backgrounds at the critical time of late adolescence and early adulthood, they have the opportunity to disrupt an insidious cycle of lifetime segregation that threatens the fabric of our pluralistic democracy" (Gurin, 1999b).

Increased Comfort Worshiping in Racially Diverse Religious Institutions

Martin Luther King described Sunday morning at 11 AM as the most segregated hour in America. More than fifty years after his death, racial segregation continues to be the norm in most religious institutions. Positive contact across racial lines has the potential to reduce this form of segregation and create more positive connections in an arena of special significance for a high percentage of the population. In a study of prior racial contact and current social ties (Emerson, Kimbro, & Yancey, 2002), investigators analyzed a large survey of "Attitudes and Social Networks" and discovered that those individuals who had experienced prior interracial contact in schools and neighborhoods were more likely, as adults, to have more racially diverse general social groups and friendship circles and were more likely to attend multiracial as opposed to uniracial religious congregations. These findings applied to Whites, African-Americans, and Hispanics. For all these groups, positive contact across racial lines increased the likelihood that individuals would choose to worship in integrated settings. Sharing the worship experience has the potential to deepen attachments and lead to a greater sense of being part of a racially diverse "community of faith."

Increase in Critical Thinking Skills

The development of critical thinking skills, defined as the ability to perceive and integrate multiple points of view, is a major educational goal. Personal contact with individuals of different racial groups enhances the development of critical thinking.

In a study conducted at three major universities (Antonio et al., 2004), White students initially filled out a questionnaire that asked about a variety of background characteristics, including the amount of interracial contact they had experienced. The students then wrote brief essays (15 minutes) on one of two social issues—child labor in developing countries or the death penalty. After writing their essays, they participated in small group discussions about the issue they had chosen. Following the discussion, the students wrote another brief essay about "their" issue, and a second brief essay about the issue they had not discussed. All three of the essays that the students wrote were rated on the degree of critical thinking demonstrated in the essay. The results were quite significant. Students who had a higher level of diverse racial contact clearly demonstrated a higher degree of critical thinking. Interacting with individuals from different racial/ethnic groups had enhanced their ability to understand and integrate multiple points of view. Segregation reinforces linear, all or nothing thinking. Integrated experiences expand one's ability to contemplate multiple ways of seeing things.

Increase in Decision Making and Problem Solving Skills

Being able to make thoughtful decisions and to solve problems in rational, constructive ways are important skills. Collaborating with individuals from different racial groups can enhance the development of these skills.

In a study of two hundred individuals who participated in twenty-nine mock juries, the functioning of homogeneously White groups was compared with that of racially diverse groups (Sommers, 2006). The findings were striking: Diverse juries deliberated longer, raised more facts about the case, and conducted broader and more wide-ranging deliberations. They also made fewer factual errors in discussing evidence, and when errors did occur those errors were more likely to be corrected during the discussion. In examining the implications of these findings, the researcher noted that:

> Because the study examines group decision-making in a realistic setting, the findings have potential implications for a variety of contexts—from the classroom to the boardroom, or wherever a premium is placed on fact-finding and reaching a good decision. Diverse groups show a number of advantages and benefits when it comes to this type of decision making.

How Does Intergroup Contact Promote Positive Change?

Positive contact, characterized by the conditions of Intergroup Contact Theory, can generate many positive changes—less stereotyping, prejudice, and discrimination; more understanding and trust; greater respect for cultural differences; and heightened critical thinking and problem solving skills. In what ways does positive contact promote these changes?

Reducing Emotional Discomfort

Children, like adults, often feel uneasy with the unfamiliar. In our highly segregated society, young people have very limited exposure to individuals who look different than themselves and different from the people they are used to encountering in their day-to-day lives. When they do encounter unfamiliar individuals or groups, they are likely to experience, consciously or unconsciously, a series of unsettling questions: "Is it safe for me to be with this person?"; "How is he seeing me?"; "What does she think about me?" "What do they expect from me?"; "Am I supposed to behave with this person (these people) in the same ways I behave with people who look like me, or are the rules different?"

Lack of "knowing," the absence of experience and guidelines, creates even more discomfort when accompanied by negative stereotypes. Research indicates that such stereotypes are often well established in children as young as three years of age (Van Ausdale & Feagin, 2001). Negative stereotypes create expectations of negative behavior. If I see you as a member of a group that I have been conditioned to believe is "mean," for example, I am likely to anticipate that you will be mean to me. If I have been conditioned to experience rejection from "your group," I will anticipate rejecting behavior. Anticipation of negative behavior is a powerful stimulus for emotional discomfort; apprehension grows in the presence of frightening expectations.

Once we are in the situation, our interpretation of what we are experiencing is also colored by our expectations. The "filter" through which I "see" you often determines *how* I see you. If I anticipate rejecting behavior, I may interpret your behavior as rejecting, even when it is not. Such an interpretation is likely to lead to a negative emotional reaction.

Contact Theory conditions create a climate in which negative expectations and emotional discomfort are diminished (Pettigrew & Tropp, 2008; Swart, Hewstone, Christ, & Voci, 2011; Tausch & Hewstone, 2010). The psychological principle of systematic desensitization is helpful in understanding how this happens. Systematic desensitization involves structured exposure over time to whatever is stimulating emotional discomfort. For example, if a person is afraid of heights, their anxiety can gradually be diminished through a series of experiences in which they are systematically exposed to greater and greater heights. In diversity initiatives, a similar process takes place. Initially, there is likely to be considerable anxiety about interacting with individuals who look different than oneself. Over time, as negative stereotypes and negative expectations are not confirmed, anxiety is diminished. When we expect members of a particular group to behave in rejecting and hostile ways and they do not do so, we begin to revise our images of what "those people" are like. After a series of positive experiences the stereotype is weakened and emotional discomfort begins to diminish—"Maybe I don't have to be afraid"; "Maybe I can let down my guard."

Experiencing Positive Emotions

In addition to creating a climate in which emotional discomfort is reduced, the Contact Theory conditions also maximize opportunities for positive emotional experiences (Pettigrew & Tropp, 2008; Tausch & Hewstone, 2010). Engaging in gratifying collaboration on shared projects produces positive feelings about the project and about the individuals with whom one is collaborating. Emotions related to "the pleasure of your company" begin to replace feelings related to you as "the unfamiliar other." Appreciation of your strengths begins to replace stereotypical notions of your limitations.

With enjoyment of shared activities and recognition of the contributions of the other person, positive images take shape and "the other" becomes an individual with particular talents, special skills, and unique personality traits. Such changes in perception can, through the psychological process of generalization, impact future reactions—thoughts, feelings, and behavior—toward other members of that individual's group. Positive experiences have the potential to challenge negative stereotypes and prompt positive expectations, not only toward the particular individuals with whom one is interacting, but also more generally toward members of that person's racial or ethnic group (Pettigrew, 1998).

Creating a Circle of Positive Change

As people feel increasingly comfortable with those who appear different from themselves, and increasingly aware of the potential for shared enjoyment, new learning, and satisfying accomplishment, they seek out more contact with one another. Positive emotions prompt a desire for additional positive interactions.

Increased contact results in growing familiarity and further identification of common interests, feelings, concerns, and life experiences. Such identification stimulates gratifying feelings of connectedness, camaraderie, and belonging. These positive feelings lead to additional positive interactions which, in turn, lead to further changes in attitudes and beliefs. Over time, an on-going "circle of positive change" is established.

Developing a Common In-Group Identity

From an early age, children develop a sense of identification with their own racial or ethnic group. Those significant others who are part of a young child's life become the foundation for that child's identity. "Who am I?" leads to: "I am like them." By preschool, most children differentiate their group (the "ingroup") from other groups that appear to be different from their own ("outgroups"). "With whom do I belong? I belong with them."

In successful diversity programs, individuals from different backgrounds develop a new aspect of identity as, over time, they experience themselves as members of a racially diverse group. This new "common ingroup identity" (Gaertner & Dovidio, 2000; Gaertner, Dovidio, Anastasio, Bachman & Rust, 1993) does not replace the original identification with their own racial or ethnic group, but rather expands their sense of self to incorporate membership in an additional, more inclusive "team." The questions of "Who am I?" and "With whom do I belong?" elicit more complex answers as the individual's world expands into increasingly diverse significant relationships.

Modeling and Identification

Indirect, observational contact leads to attitudinal and behavioral change through the psychological processes of modeling and identification. When members of different groups interact in cooperative and friendly ways, they provide positive models for observers from each of their groups. Observing positive interactions reduces anxiety and promotes identification– "if they can do this, maybe it would be OK for me to do it too." In addition, observation of friendly intergroup contact can reduce stereotypes—"Maybe those people aren't so angry, aloof, etc.; maybe I was wrong about them."

Summary and Conclusions

The research is compelling. Positive contact between individuals from different racial groups has many important benefits: reduction in stereotypes and prejudice; increased comfort and confidence interacting with people whose racial background is different from one's own; improvement in workplace performance; decrease in residential segregation; increase in racially inclusive religious worship; enhanced development of critical thinking, decision-making, and problem-solving skills. For young people, intergroup contact is essential for the development of knowledge and skills necessary for living and working in an increasingly diverse world.

Many studies have demonstrated that the most effective contact is that which conforms to some or all of the conditions identified by Gordon Allport in his historic formulation of Intergroup Contact Theory. These conditions form the framework for our discussion of diversity initiatives for children, adolescents, and adults.

References

Allport, G. W. (1954). *The nature of prejudice*. Cambridge, MA: Addison-Wesley.

Amicus brief of 553 Social Scientists in Support of School Integration, October 4, 2006.

Antonio, A. L., Chang, M. J., Hakuta, K., Kenny, D. A., Levin, S. & Milem, J. F. (2004). Effects of racial diversity on complex thinking in college students. *Psychological Science, 15*(8), 507–510.

Chang, M. J., Astin, A. W. & Kim, D. (2004). Cross-racial interaction among undergraduates: Some consequences, causes, and patterns. *Research in Higher Education, 45*(5), 529–553.

Civil Rights Project. (2002). *The impact of racial and ethnic diversity on educational outcomes: Cambridge MA school district*. Cambridge, MA: Harvard University, Civil Rights Project.

Davies, K., Tropp, L. R., Aron, A., Pettigrew, T. F., & Wright, S. C. (2011). Cross-group friendships and intergroup attitudes: a meta-analytic review. *Personality and Social Psychology Review, 15*(4), 332–351.

Eaton, S. E. (2001). *The other Boston busing story: What's won and lost across the boundaryline*. New Haven, CT: Yale University Press.

Emerson, M. O., Kimbro, R. T. & Yancey, G. (2002). Contact theory extended: The effects of prior racial contact on current social ties. *Social Science Quarterly, 83*(3), 745–761.

Fischer, M. J. (2008). Does campus diversity promote friendship diversity? A look at interracial friendships in college. *Social Science Quarterly, 89*(3), 631–655.

Fischer v. University of Texas at Austin (November 2, 2015). Amicus brief of fortune 100 and other leading American businesses.

Gaertner, S. L. & Dovidio, J. F. (2000). *Reducing intergroup bias: The common ingroup identity model*. Philadelphia, PA: Psychology Press.

Gaertner, S. L., Dovidio, J. F., Anastasio, P. A., Bachman, B.A. & Rust, M. C. (1993). The common ingroup identity model: Recategorization and the reduction of intergroup bias. *European Review of Social Psychology*, 4(1), 1–26.

Gurin, P. (1999a). Expert reports in defense of University of Michigan: Expert report of Patricia Gurin. *Equity and Excellence in Education, 32*(2), 36–62.

Gurin, P. (1999b). Expert testimony in Gratz, et al. v. Bollinger, et al. & Grutter, et al. v. Bollinger, et al., in The Compelling Need for Diversity in Higher Education. Ann Arbor: University of Michigan. www.vpcomm.umich.edu/admissions/research

Harwood, J. (2016). Music and intergroup communication. *Oxford Research Encyclopedia of Communication*, communication.oxfordre.com

Killen, M., Crystal, D.S. & Ruck, M. (2007). The social developmental benefits of intergroup contact among children and adolescents. In F. Frankenberg & G. Orfield (Eds.), *Lessons in integration: Realizing the promise of racial diversity in American schools* (pp. 57–73). Charlottesville, VA: University of Virginia Press.

Kurlaender, M., & Yun, J. T. (2007). Measuring school racial composition and student outcomes in a multiracial society. *American Journal of Education, 113*(2), 213–242.

Miles, E., & Crisp, R. J. (2014). A meta-analytic test of the imagined contact hypothesis. *Group Processes and Intergroup Relations, 17*(1), 3–26.

Pettigrew, T. (1998). Intergroup contact theory. *Annual Review of Psychology, 49, 65–85.*

Pettigrew, T. F., & Tropp, L. R. (2006). A meta-analytic test of intergroup contact theory. *Journal of Personality & Social Psychology, 90*(5), 751–783.

Pettigrew, T. F., & Tropp, L. R. (2008). How does intergroup contact reduce prejudice? Meta-analytic tests of three mediators. *European Journal of Social Psychology, 38*(6), 922–934.

Saha, S., Guiton, G., Wimmers, P. F. & Wilkerson, L. (2008). Student body racial and ethnic composition and diversity-related outcomes in US medical schools. *JAMA, 300*(10), 1135–1145.

Schiappa, E., Gregg, P. B., & Hewes, D. E. (2006). Can one TV show make a difference? *Will & Grace* and the parasocial contact hypothesis. *Journal of Homosexuality, 51*(4), 15–37.

Schofield, J. W. (1995). Review of research on school desegregation's impact on elementary and secondary school students. In J. A. Banks & C. A. McGee Banks (Eds.), *Handbook of research on multicultural education* (pp. 597–617). New York: Macmillan.

Sommers, S. R. (2006). On racial diversity and group decision making: Identifying multiple effects of racial composition on jury deliberations. *Journal of Personality and Social Psychology, 90*(4), 597–612.

Swart, H., Hewstone, M., Christ, O. & Voci, A. (2011). Affective mediators of intergroup contact: A three-wave longitudinal study in South Africa. *Journal of Personality and Social Psychology, 101.* 1221–1238.

Tausch, N., & Hewstone, M. (2010). Intergroup contact. In J. F. Dovidio, M. Hewstone, P. Glick, & V. M. Esses (Eds.), *The Sage handbook of prejudice, stereotyping, and discrimination* (pp. 544–560). Thousand Oaks, CA: Sage.

United States Census Bureau News Release (May 17, 2012). Most children younger than age 1 are minorities.

Van Ausdale, D., & Feagin, J. R. (2001). *The first R: How children learn race and racism.* Lanham, MD: Rowman & Littlefield.

Wells, A. S., Duran, J. S., & White, T. (2008). Refusing to leave desegregation behind: From graduates of racially diverse schools to the Supreme Court. *Teachers College Record,* 110(12), 2532–2570.

Wells, A. S., & Frankenberg, E. (2007). The public schools and the challenge of the Supreme Court's integration decision. *Phi Delta Kappan,* 89(3), 178–188.

Wright, S. C., Aron, A., McLaughlin-Volpe, T., & Ropp, S. A. (1997). The extended contact effect: Knowledge of cross group friendships and prejudice. *Journal of Personality and Social Psychology,* 73(1), 73–90.

Chapter 2

Two Diversity Programs for Children, Teens, and Families

In 1963, Dr. Martin Luther King, Jr. described his now-famous dream, imagining a world in which: "little Black boys and Black girls will be able to join hands with little White boys and little White girls as sisters and brothers (Washington, 1986)." In the highly segregated environment of Southwest Michigan, Dr. King's dream can seem a distant vision, a faraway goal, perhaps naïve and unattainable. But on a snowy morning in March 2005, a more hopeful picture was emerging. The All God's Children Community Choir, a racially diverse group of girls and boys, ranging in age from 3 to 12, had been invited to perform for 2,500 educators at the big convention center in Grand Rapids. Children, parents, and choir directors would need to leave by 7:45 AM in order to arrive on time for the opening ceremony. At 7:30, the bus driver began to express serious doubts about the likelihood that families would come out through a blizzard on an early Saturday morning to make such a trip. But come they did—in cars, in vans, in pickup trucks; inching forward, headlights peeking through the snow. By 7:45 the bus was filled with exuberant riders. Six cars carrying additional children and parents lined up behind the bus, ready to follow in tandem. As the bus driver prepared to start the journey, one of the choir directors suggested a "word of prayer," and a choir dad took the microphone at the front of the bus. "We're the All God's Children Choir, Lord, and we're asking your blessing for safe passage through this storm so we can take our message to the teachers in Grand Rapids." As Brother Brown spoke, row after row of Black and White children reached out to each other, side by side and across the aisle, joining hands as "sisters and brothers." In the tenderness of that moment, Dr. King's dream didn't seem so far away after all.

Martin Luther King dreamed of a world in which race would no longer be a barrier, a world where children from different racial groups would come to know one another as individuals, rather than stereotypes. Dr. King believed that if significant numbers of children and families could reach across the racial divide and learn to live together in harmony they might be able to create, over time, "Beloved Communities" of mutual understanding, respect, and trust.

There was little evidence of Beloved Community in author Alex Kotlowitz's 1998 depiction of Southwest Michigan (Kotlowitz, 1998). In *The Other Side of the River*, Kotlowitz described the jarring discrepancies between the "twin cities" of Benton Harbor and St. Joseph, which sit side by side, separated only by a river. St. Joseph, a middle to upper class community, is more than 90% White. Benton Harbor, one of the most economically depressed towns in the United States, is more than 90% Black. Kotlowitz pointed out that the segregation, economic inequality, alienation, hostility, and mistrust that exist between these two communities are representative of the state of race relations throughout America.

In response to Kotlowitz's book, approximately one hundred racially diverse residents of Southwest Michigan came together to create new organizations dedicated to promoting positive social change. Two of these organizations, the Race Relations Council and Twin Cities Together, became instrumental in the development of long-lasting diversity initiatives for children and teens. These initiatives, the *All God's Children Community Choir* and *Calling All Colors of Southwest Michigan*, illustrate the many ways that diversity programs can make a difference in the lives of children, adolescents, families, and communities.

The All God's Children Community Choir

One of the first programs initiated by the Race Relations Council was a Community Celebration and Awards Program, designed to honor the achievements of local pioneers and "unsung heroes," from both sides of the river, who had made important contributions to earlier efforts to promote racial justice and racial healing. The goal was not only to pay tribute to valuable role models but also to prompt a shift away from pervasive negativity and toward a more hopeful vision of what is possible. In addition to profiling the award winners, the event also included uplifting musical entertainment. For the first two years of the Awards Program, this entertainment was provided by professional singers and musicians. In planning for the third year, the organizing committee had a different idea—why not bring together a diverse group of children from Benton Harbor and St. Joseph to form a multiracial choir; why not model, through the entertainment itself, a different picture of Southwest Michigan? The two of us volunteered to coordinate this effort. We envisioned significant benefits, not only for the audience, but also for the participants themselves. We hoped that by collaborating on a meaningful project, children and families from different racial groups, usually separated by distance and mistrust, would come to know one another as individuals. We believed that over time, stereotypes and prejudice would diminish, mutual understanding and respect would increase, and friendships between the children and their families would develop.

Once the vision was in place, we sought the assistance of two local ministers, each of whom had been supportive of the Race Relations Council's efforts. One minister was based in Benton Harbor, with an exclusively Black congregation; the other was in St. Joseph, with a congregation that was entirely White. The ministers put us in touch with their children's choir directors, who agreed to recruit volunteers for the new community choir, and to serve as part of the choir's multiracial leadership team. Twenty children, and families, from each church signed on—the "All God's Children Community Choir" was becoming a reality.

In launching the choir we wanted the adults "in charge" to reflect the diversity of the members and their families. We believed that each child would benefit from seeing "someone who looks like me" directing the group and assuming a respected role on the leadership team. If the choir were to model diversity, its own structure needed to reflect that diversity.

At the first rehearsal, children and families from each community initially stayed very close to those they knew. They clustered with their friends, their eyes scanning their surroundings. Adults and children alike appeared curious, but more than a little wary. Once the rehearsal itself was underway, and the focus shifted to singing, everyone began to relax. All participants had been provided with audiotapes of several songs, with themes of friendship, peace, and respect for all people. Because of the tapes, everyone began from the same starting point, and the familiarity of the music helped to set the children at ease. They joined together in common purpose, refining the same songs and enjoying the playful exchanges between the multiracial team of directors.

Gathering later for lunch, however, it was striking to see that children and families again divided into racially homogeneous clusters. Each group stayed with those who looked most like them; everyone relied on their preexisting, "safe," relationships. After about fifteen minutes some of the younger children, spurred on by curiosity and restlessness, began to disregard the unspoken "boundaries." Three 5 year olds drifted over to adjacent tables as pizza was being served. One boy from St. Joseph, realizing there were no pepperoni slices on his cheese pizza, was quick to express his disappointment: "I didn't get any circles on my piece." The Benton Harbor boy next to him sprang into action. Pulling two "circles" from his own pizza, he gently popped them into his neighbor's mouth. The boys exchanged grins, and proceeded to "hang out" together for the rest of the afternoon.

Following their lead, several other children began talking and playing together. Teenagers and parents were more hesitant, but when the time came to clean up, everyone pitched in and worked together. The overall climate seemed to shift from wary separation to tentative engagement. Emotional discomfort was beginning to give way to positive anticipation of future encounters. All participants had successfully navigated unfamiliar waters and had gathered some new, reassuring data about their "neighbors" from the other side of the river.

The audiotapes of songs about brotherhood and sisterhood, unity, and peace insured that at the first rehearsal the children had something in common. Everyone had started to learn the same songs, everyone had been introduced to the same value-laden messages. By the end of that first practice they had something else in common—newly designed t-shirts emblazoned with the words ALL GOD'S CHILDREN upon a multicolored rainbow measure of music. The notes on that music appeared in the form of children's faces reflecting a wide variety of racial/ethnic backgrounds.

Following the initial gathering, a series of rehearsals was held, alternating between the two churches that had volunteered participants. In early contacts anxiety was apparent in the faces of both children and adults from each community, anxiety about going to "the other side of the river," anxiety about dealing with people who looked "different than me and my neighbors." After a few rehearsals, however, the anxiety began to dissipate, and everyone appeared to feel increasingly relaxed about being in unfamiliar territory.

Three months after their first encounter, the All God's Children Community Choir had its debut performance at the Third Annual Race Relations Council Awards Program. Even before the choir members began to sing, it was clear they were having an impact on the audience. As this diverse group of children filed into the hall, proudly wearing their new choir shirts, there was an audible gasp of surprise and delight from the crowd. Once on the risers, the children sang with enthusiasm, and by the time they began their concluding song, the audience members were on their feet, clapping and joining the chorus of "Keep a little light, burning bright, in your heart, night and day." The choir was launched, and soon afterward requests for future engagements began pouring in. We were delighted, and hopeful that the All God's Children Community Choir could be an abiding presence in Southwest Michigan!

In the following nineteen years, the Choir has expanded in age, from 3–12 to 4–18, as many older choir members stayed on board through their middle and high school years. In addition, new children and teens have been drawn to the choir after seeing a performance or at the urging of a friend already active in the group. In order to give special recognition and special opportunities to the older children, the choir formed a "Teen and Pre-Teen Ensemble" for everyone age 10 or older. At each rehearsal the directors work with the older group exclusively for one hour, giving them an opportunity for input on song selection and for the refinement of more complex music. In the second hour the younger children join the older ones and the full choir rehearses for an additional hour. In performances, the older group usually "opens the show" by performing one or two songs. They are then joined on stage by the younger children and the full choir performs for the remainder of the program. On occasion, the older group alone has been sought out for a particular event—for example, an evening concert that would end too late for the younger children or a combined concert with a middle and high school summer music camp, performing songs in many languages.

The racial mix has become more diversified with the addition of several Asian-American and Hispanic children and their families. The Choir's repertoire has grown to include songs in Spanish and Zulu, as well as the English, Hebrew, and Swahili songs of the early days.

All God's Children rehearses two or more times each month, at a variety of locations throughout the region. In traveling from place to place, children and families have expanded their sense of community. Over time, much of the uneasiness, often felt in Southwest Michigan when residents leave their familiar, largely segregated neighborhoods, has quieted. For this group, rehearsing in varied locations on both sides of the river has led to an increased ease of movement, growing comfort and acceptance, and a feeling that "we all *belong* everywhere."

In addition to local churches and libraries, choir practices are sometimes scheduled at special locations that expand the children's horizons—for example, the local children's museum during an exhibit on the biology of skin color; the local art museum during a special photography exhibit on racial and ethnic diversity; the local Montessori school during spring "birthing time" on the school farm. These "special" practices provide an opportunity for choir members and their families to share a variety of engaging experiences and to discuss their reactions to those experiences in a relaxed setting over a common meal.

Choir rehearsals always begin with five to ten minutes of "gathering time," during which children and families greet and check in with one another. Though many in the group have been together for years, everyone makes a name tag, which they wear throughout the rehearsal; name recognition is an important part of the "getting-to-know-one another" process, and name tags are very helpful when new members join the choir. At times the children may create a get-well poster for a choir member or parent who is ill, a welcome poster for a guest artist in an upcoming concert, or a thank-you poster for the church, library, museum, etc. that is hosting the rehearsal on that day.

At the end of each rehearsal there is an opportunity for choir members to share "announcements" about their achievements, large and small—school honors, sports accomplishments, play performances, dance recitals, etc. Following announcements everyone shares a meal, planned and prepared by choir parents and grandparents. Over time, it has become clear that the camaraderie that develops around food is especially valuable. There is often laughter, sharing of recipes, and animated conversation coming from the kitchen. Many informal exchanges occur, and children and adults often discover a variety of shared interests and concerns. Once a month the meal ends with a celebration of choir birthdays. Several years ago some parents and grandparents began, quite spontaneously, joining the birthday line-up. This development has deepened the feeling, among children and adults, that All God's Children has become much like an extended family.

Periodically, the choir schedules events that are "just for fun"—hayrides, swim parties, attending a play or dance performance together. These informal gatherings give children, teens, and adults an opportunity to broaden their relationships and to model for the wider community the benefits of friendship across racial lines.

In order to avoid any issues of financial inequality, there are no fees associated with membership in All God's Children, and a "choir fund" covers all expenses. Contributions to the choir fund have come from the Race Relations Council, local businesses and foundations, audience members, friends, organizations sponsoring specific performances, and voluntary, anonymous contributions from some choir families and their relatives. Choir shirts and vests, meals, birthday cakes, charter buses, hotel rooms, and tickets for family members to attend choir performances and special events have all been paid for by the choir fund. When rising gas prices began to limit some families' ability to travel to rehearsals and performances, a "transportation fund" was created, allowing those families to receive, anonymously, financial assistance for travel expenses when needed.

Since its creation, All God's Children has performed on more than 150 occasions. The highlights include:

- Yearly appearances at Lake Michigan College to commemorate the birthday of Dr. Martin Luther King, Jr.
- Multiple performances at Artsbridge, an inspiring program of the First Presbyterian churches of Benton Harbor and Buchanan, Michigan, designed to bring people together from many different communities to share experiences in the arts.
- A special Habitat for Humanity performance for former President Jimmy Carter
- Concerts in Grand Rapids and Traverse City for state and national teachers' conferences
- Joint appearances with the Chicago Children's Choir, in Michigan and in Chicago
- A holiday concert with the Southwest Michigan Symphony Orchestra and Metropolitan Opera Star Angela Brown
- A featured performance on Navy Pier in Chicago to commemorate Martin Luther King day.
- Performances with renowned professional musicians Tom Chapin, Josh White, Jr., Gemini, LaRon Williams, Nikki Harris, Peter Yarrow, Ben Vereen, and Pamela Chappell (with whom All God's Children recorded an award-winning CD).
- A choir CD, titled All God's Children, released in January, 2013 and a Teen Ensemble CD, released in January, 2016.

Performances provide exciting opportunities for the children to bring their music and their message to local and, on occasion, distant communities. Each appearance has been a bonding experience for everyone involved. Sharing the enthusiasm around "putting on a show" fuels a sense of common purpose, a feeling of being members of the same team. Sharing the "afterglow"—the applause, admiration, and appreciation from the audience, reinforces the feeling that "*we* are making a difference."

In addition to rehearsals and performances, choir families and choir directors sometimes celebrate holidays and special events together, and periodically help one another through difficult times. Some families attend concerts, plays, sports events, and church programs with one another; some exchange "play dates," birthday parties and sleepovers. Teen choir members have helped one another prepare for driver's license exams and supported candidates for the local Blossom-time King and Queen pageant. When choir families have encountered medical, employment, or financial crises, other families have sometimes "stepped in" to provide support in a variety of ways—for example, a month of homemade meals delivered postsurgery; chain restaurant gift certificates donated to a family traveling for medical treatments; tech support provided for a parent with new demands on the job; a "rebuild team" that showed up to help repair a family's horse shelter toppled by winter storms. All of these experiences have deepened the connections between choir members, parents and grandparents. Over time, trust and a sense of belonging have developed. Racial differences are certainly still apparent, but individuals are increasingly recognized for their unique characteristics, rather than their race. Stereotypes have diminished, and there is an overarching "we" feeling that embraces differences and celebrates our common bond.

The larger community benefits as audiences enjoy the choir's performances, absorb the message of their music, and observe the warm, comfortable relationships that have developed between the choir children, their families, and the choir directors. Audience members often report feeling "inspired" and "deeply moved" by what they have seen and heard; they comment that the All God's Children Community

Choir represents a "different vision" of life in Southwest Michigan, a "more hopeful one."

Calling All Colors of Southwest Michigan

Within the same time period that the All God's Children Community Choir was being launched, a second, and quite different, diversity initiative for children began in Southwest Michigan. This program, Calling All Colors, was originally developed at Coastal Carolina University in response to a crisis situation. In 1991, prompted by mounting racial tensions in their area, Coastal Carolina held a conference on "Healing the Wounds of Racism: Education's Role." A few days after the conference, nine-year old Anisa Kinz, a fourth grade student at a local elementary school, went with her mother to talk with the Dean of Community and Graduate Education at the university. Anisa suggested holding a second conference, this time for elementary school children. "After all," she said, "children are the future and new attitudes should start with us." The Dean was taken with Anisa's idea, and together they organized a group of children and adults to create the first Calling All Colors program, a one-day gathering in which children from different racial groups came together to share a variety of activities and begin to know one another in a relaxed, safe environment.

The Southwest Michigan Calling All Colors initiative began by following the original once-a-year format, but soon evolved into a larger and more comprehensive program. In the Southwest Michigan evolution of the program, predominantly Black elementary school classrooms from Benton Harbor are paired with predominantly White same-grade classrooms from St. Joseph. The children initially come together for two half-days, three to four weeks apart, and share carefully crafted activities designed to diminish anxiety, challenge stereotypes, and increase mutual understanding and respect.

Program days begin with an opening assembly in which students sit with their own classmates and are introduced to themes of the day by Calling All Colors staff. The staff members use age-appropriate humor to identify important concepts and to alleviate the obvious tension as the groups scrutinize their counterparts from "the other side of the river." For example, an opening presentation may include "A Walk in Somebody Else's Shoes." Student volunteers from each class are given a variety of ill-fitting adult shoes and asked to walk across the room together. Participants and observers alike break into giggles as they experience the awkwardness on display. Well-placed commentary from the facilitator makes the point: "It's not always easy to walk in another person's shoes. We have to put in some extra effort. And that's what we'll be doing today…having fun and putting in some effort to learn about each other."

At the close of the opening assembly, each child is assigned to a mixed group of 8 to 12 (half from each school), and within that group everyone is linked to a "buddy" from the other school. These small groups, led by a trained facilitator (or pair of facilitators) will be the hub of the day's interactive activities. The more intimate connection with a buddy provides the opportunity to discover similarities and differences and to develop more personal camaraderie.

At the heart of the Calling All Colors program is a series of meaningful shared small group activities. One activity that is often used at the beginning of small group time is a name-learning circle game, in which each child says his or her name and favorite food. The group links the name with the food in a rhythmic clapping chant that eventually includes everyone in the circle ("Ice cream Larry, Pizza Patty, Sweet potato Sandy, etc"). In addition to helping the children learn each other's names, the activity prompts beginning recognition of similarities that cross the racial divide ("Pizza is my favorite, too!"). Another activity, often saved for the end of small-group time, is called "Diversity Beans." The children select a treat from a brightly-colored array of jelly beans, and each offers his or her best guess about the flavor they've chosen. The beans that have been provided are made in such a way that the color on the outside does not match the flavor on the inside (e.g., the yellow bean may be cherry, the red bean may be licorice). As the children simultaneously bite into the beans there are giggles and exclamations of surprise. A lively discussion follows regarding jumping to conclusions and making judgments based on outward appearance—

"Do we always know what's on the inside by how things look on the outside?"; "Can we always guess what our experience will be based on what we see?"

Toward the end of small group time, the children gather in a circle to talk about the experience. The facilitator asks a question to get the discussion started. For example, one facilitator asked the following question to a group of third-graders: "This day was probably different than what you are used to. When anyone is going into a new situation, they usually try to 'get ready' by imagining what it will be like. Was today just as you imagined it would be or was it different? Was there anything about today that surprised you?" After a few moments of quiet reflection, one Benton Harbor student pointed to his "buddy" from St. Joseph and said: "I was surprised he *liked* me." The buddy's response was: "I was surprised you liked *me*." This led to a chorus of similar responses from other children from both communities; each child had anticipated rejection. The children talked openly about their expectations, their relief at finding acceptance, and their excitement about the discovery of common interests, likes, and dislikes. It was clear that they were eagerly anticipating being with their new friends at the next Calling All Colors gathering.

After the small group experience, a closing assembly brings everyone back together. The change in the emotional climate is striking! The same children who eyed each other warily as they disembarked from their school buses earlier in the day often return from their small groups chatting amiably, with their arms draped casually over the shoulders of their new-found friends. One African-American boy from Benton Harbor had initially said to his classmate as they entered the building and saw the children from St. Joseph: "White kids? I hate White kids!" At the end of the day, as the children were getting ready to return to their school buses, he said to that same classmate: "Hey, I got me a White friend."

The classroom teachers expand on and reinforce the Calling All Colors experience by following up with pen pal letters, e-mail exchanges, classroom visits, and other forms of on-going contact. In addition, the teachers organize discussions about some of the issues raised by Calling All Colors. In one classroom, each student wrote an essay describing their thoughts and feelings about the Calling All Colors program.

At the end of the school year all of the children who participated in Calling All Colors, as well as their parents, are invited to a family picnic. This event provides a valuable opportunity for families to share an experience in a relaxed, informal setting. There are games and music, and everyone enjoys a buffet picnic supper. The children play together and parents are drawn into lively interactions—coaching and judging musical chairs, joining in group singing, serving food, etc. The children's previous Calling All Colors connections provide a point of entry for their parents. Barriers of race and class begin to dissipate during the course of this warm communal experience.

Students participate in Calling All Colors at four different grade levels—first, second, third, and fourth. By the time the children enter middle school, they have had four consecutive years of exposure to the benefits that the Calling All Colors program provides.

As Calling All Colors has grown in Southwest Michigan, curriculum modules have been created for the students at each participating grade level, and training sessions have been developed for classroom teachers and program facilitators. Calling All Colors facilitators establish a safe environment in which the children can meet, collaborate in small groups on shared projects, talk openly about racial differences and similarities, and begin to know each other as individuals.

In the first year of the Southwest Michigan Calling All Colors program there were one hundred and twenty student participants. By the second year, the number had risen to two hundred and fifty, and by the third year there were close to six hundred participants. Over time, the numbers have continued to grow—there are now more than a thousand students in the program each school year!

Calling All Colors offers an important opportunity for children from different racial backgrounds to come together in positive, meaningful ways. During the course of their participation the discomfort with "the other" shifts as each stranger becomes an individual with whom one has worked on a common task, shared enjoyable activities, and, at times, talked with about difficult feelings and experiences. The children discover that, despite their differences, they have much in common. They may share the excitement of performing in a dance recital, playing rocket football, or welcoming a new baby into their family. They may also share the frustration of dealing with a "bossy" older sibling, the fear of starting a new school, or the pain of being picked last in gym class. As they discuss similar interests, preferences, and challenges, they come to know each other in an increasingly personal way; stereotypes give way to reality. Interactions are less guarded, more spontaneous. There is more laughter, more demonstrative behavior, more sharing of confidences.

The families of Calling All Colors participants benefit by talking with their children about the experience and by noting changes in attitudes and behavior. Parents have described chance encounters in shopping malls, skating rinks, soccer games, etc., and remarked on the ease and warm familiarity evident between children who have participated in the same Calling All Colors small groups. During the course of the elementary school years, such encounters become increasingly common.

Parents also benefit from the end-of-the year family picnic. Their direct experience of children and parents from "the other side of the river" helps to reduce stereotypes and prejudice and provides a context for parents to begin to know one another as individuals.

In Southwest Michigan, teachers and school administrators have been enthusiastic supporters of the Calling All Colors program. They recognize the critical importance of diversity education for the children in their schools and see Calling All Colors as a valuable addition to the curriculum. Administrators have provided free bus transportation from their schools and have encouraged their teachers to participate in the program. Teachers have expressed appreciation that Calling All Colors has "broken the ice" and stimulated important classroom discussions about previously "taboo" subjects related to race and ethnicity.

The impact of Calling All Colors has expanded as community organizations have periodically formed partnerships with the program in order to advance shared goals. The local children's museum, *Curious Kids*, invited Calling All Colors participants to brainstorm with their staff about possible ideas for a new exhibit on skin color. Following a morning of Calling All Colors activities focused on the role of melanin in determining skin color, the children went with their buddies to the museum, eager to be helpful. With much enthusiasm they volunteered a host of creative ideas, and museum staff drew liberally from their input. Two fourth-grade buddies suggested: "Why don't you make two models of the human body, one with white skin and one with brown skin, and have the models open up so everyone can see that even though they're different on the outside, they're the same on the inside?" The students' idea became the wellspring for a new exhibit, "Inside Out—The Skin We're In," the first children's museum exhibit in the country to focus specifically on skin color.

In addition to the benefits provided to local children, families, schools, and community organizations, the Southwest Michigan Calling All Colors program has become a resource for communities in other parts of the country. In August, 2007, four representatives of the program (the director, a group facilitator, and the authors, who are Calling All Colors consultants and board members) were invited to Northern Arizona University in Flagstaff to introduce the Calling All Colors experience to a local community group. Faculty members from the Martin-Springer Institute assembled a diverse group of community leaders who had expressed concerns about the divisions in their area and interest in what might be working in other parts of the country. The predominant racial/ethnic groups in the Flagstaff community are different than those in Southwest Michigan (Mexican-American, Native American, and White populations rather than predominantly Black and White) but the problems are strikingly similar—rigid separation, economic inequality, alienation, and mistrust. In an intensive two-day workshop the principles and techniques of the Calling All Colors approach were presented and discussed, and efforts were made to tailor the program to meet the needs of the local community. As the workshop concluded, the Flagstaff organizers were energized, speaking with much excitement about the potential impact of Calling All Colors in their part of the country. The initial groundwork was established, and a new initiative was launched.

Two Complementary Approaches

The All God's Children Choir and the Calling All Colors program represent two different, but complementary, approaches to building bridges across the racial divide. Each approach has its own particular strengths and limitations. All God's Children provides more contact over a longer period of time in a greater variety of settings, and includes more direct family involvement. Calling All Colors involves a much larger number of participants and provides an important diversity education component to school curricula. Children, families, and communities all benefit from each approach; the benefits multiply significantly when both formats are available.

There are many variations on these two models. In some communities, instead of a multiracial choir there might be a multiracial dance troupe, drama group, artists' club, or athletic program. Rather than the Calling All Colors format, there might be a diversity education program that focuses primarily on weekend retreats or shared field trips. All of these variations are based on the same fundamental principle: positive inter-group contact leads to a reduction in stereotypes and prejudice and an increase in mutual understanding, respect, and trust.

References

Kotlowitz, A. (1998). *The other side of the river: A story of two towns, a death, and America's dilemma.* New York: Nan A. Talese/Doubleday.

Washington, J. M. (Ed.). (1986). *A testament of hope: The essential writings of Martin Luther King, Jr.* San Francisco: Harper & Row.

Chapter 3

Bridge Building Activities for Children, Teens, and Families

There are a large number of activities that parents, teachers, schools, and communities can pursue to help children and adolescents build bridges across the racial divide. In this chapter we explore a variety of these activities.

Modeling

Parents

In most circumstances, parents are children's first role models. Children observe their parents' verbal and nonverbal behavior and identify (consciously or unconsciously) with what they observe. If parents model stereotyping and prejudice, their children are likely to internalize those attitudes. If parents behave in ways that challenge stereotypes and counter prejudice, their children are likely to follow their lead (Degner & Dalege, 2013).

What parents *do* is more important than what they *say*. This phenomenon is illustrated in a study of European-American mothers and their young children (Pahlke, Bigler, & Suizzo, 2012). The study ex-amined the children's and mothers' expressed racial attitudes and the mothers' self-reported friendship group. The researchers found that the children's attitudes were not significantly related to their mother's attitudes, but there was a significant relationship between the chil-dren's attitudes and their mother's friendship group. Those children whose mothers had a higher percentage of Non-White friends dem-onstrated less racial bias than did those children whose mothers had a lower percentage of Non-White friends. Children internalize what they observe. If they observe friendships between their parents and people from different racial backgrounds, they are likely to think, consciously or unconsciously: "If this is who you feel safe with, who you seek out for enjoyment and support in difficult times, then these must be people of value."

When parents have a more narrowly homogeneous friendship group, children are less likely to develop more inclusive attitudes and behaviors. An example of this dynamic occurred in Oak Park, Illinois, a community just outside of Chicago that for many years has been mak-ing a strong effort to create and sustain a racially integrated community. A group of Oak Park parents noticed that their children had embraced diverse friendship groups in elementary school, but by the time they reached high school their friendship group was racially homogeneous. They asked their teenagers for an explanation. The teens replied: "You talk about the importance of integration, but all of your close friends—the people you spend the most time with—are the same race as you. Your behavior doesn't match your words." The parents were not ex-pecting this reply, but when they thought about what their children had said, they saw the inconsistency between their words and their behavior. In response, they decided to form a group—Project Unity, designed to bring together adults from different racial backgrounds to discuss race-related issues and provide opportunities for social interac-tion and the development of authentic friendships. The initiative was a success, and soon there were multiple Project Unity groups meeting regularly once a month. The gap between the adults' words and their behavior was beginning to narrow.

Teachers

With the exception of parents, teachers are usually the most important adult influences on children's social development. What teachers
model about equality has significant impact on children's attitudes and
behavior regarding race (Suttie, 2016).

There are many ways for teachers to model a commitment to racial
equality, and we will review a variety of these in this section. Initially, though, we want to focus on the importance of teachers becoming
aware of their own *implicit biases*, their unconscious assumptions about
how race influences behavior. Everyone has such biases, though most
people are not conscious of them. In order for teachers to effectively
model bridge-building behavior, they need to address and modify their
own implicit racial biases.

The presence of unconscious racial assumptions was demonstrated
in a recent study of preschool teachers (Gilliam, Maupin, Reyes, Accavitti, & Shic, 2016). The teachers were asked to look for behavioral
problems in a video of a preschool class with Black and White children,
none of whom were actually exhibiting behavioral problems. The researchers filmed the teachers' eye movements while they were watching the video. They found that the teachers spent considerably more
time looking at the Black boys in the class than any other group. White
boys were the second most watched group. The teachers clearly had an
implicit bias that boys, and especially Black boys, were most likely to
misbehave.

Implicit biases influence perception—we see what we expect to see.
Biased perceptions can lead to biased reactions. Teachers who unconsciously assume that African-American boys are the ones most likely
to have behavioral problems are more likely to perceive misbehavior
from this group. These perceptions, in turn, are likely to lead to more
interventions and harsher discipline. Implicit bias is almost certainly
one reason that African-American boys are disciplined and excluded
from school much more often than any other group (U.S. Dept. of Education, 2014).

How can teachers reduce their unconscious biases? The first step is
acknowledging that such biases exist. This is not an easy thing to do.

Teachers, like most people, want to believe that their behavior is "color blind," that they approach all children with the same, stereotype-free perspective. As a result, they are often resistant to acknowledging their implicit racial biases. If, however, they are willing to make a commitment to increasing their awareness of these phenomena, important changes can take place.

In a recent study (Morewedge, et al., 2015), participants received a training intervention, which consisted of either playing a computer game or watching an instructional video, both of which were designed to increase awareness of a variety of forms of implicit bias—*Blind Spot Bias (seeing bias in others but not in yourself); Confirmation Bias (interpreting new information as confirmation of your own pre-existing beliefs); Fundamental Attribution Error (assuming that negative behavior by people like yourself is primarily a result of social circumstances while negative behavior by people who seem different from yourself is primarily the result of their "character"); Anchoring Bias (relying too much on initial impressions); Representativeness (judging people by how much they fit your internal representation of a particular kind of person); and Social Projection (assuming that other people agree with your view of the world).* The results of the study showed that both the computer game and the video were effective techniques for reducing implicit racial bias.

In addition to increased awareness of unconscious bias, two other processes can help teachers model racial equality in the classroom:

1) Increasing Empathic Understanding
Teachers and students can both benefit greatly when teachers take the time to learn about the lived experience of their students. Empathic "perspective taking"—vicariously experiencing another's feelings and point of view—has been shown to decrease stereotypical views of others (Todd, Bodenhausen, & Galinsky, 2012).

A study of empathy training for teachers (Okanoufa, Paunesku, & Walton, 2016) found that after the training the frequency of student suspensions (which are disproportionately high for racial minority students) was greatly reduced. The researchers examined the effects of encouraging teachers to adopt an "empathic mindset about discipline," which they defined as one that "prioritizes valuing and understanding students' experiences and the negative feelings that give rise to misbehavior, sustaining positive relationships with misbehaving students, and working with students within trusting relationships to improve behavior." Thirty-one middle school teachers participated in online learning experiences focused on encouraging them to adopt an empathic mindset. They first read an article that described "nonpejorative reasons why students sometimes misbehave in class and how positive relationships with teachers can facilitate students' growth." They then read stories from students that reinforced an empathic mindset. A brief excerpt from one of these stories: "One day I got detention, and instead of just sitting there, my teacher talked with me about what happened. He really listened to me. … It felt good to know I had someone I could trust in school. …" After reading these stories, the teachers wrote essays about how they could incorporate an empathic mindset into their own teaching.

Two months after the initial training, the teachers received a second round of empathy-building experiences. They were reminded that "students' feelings about and behavior in school can and do improve when teachers successfully convey the care and respect that students crave." They read a story from a teacher who talked about how one of her own teachers had shown her respect and how she tried to do the same with her students. The participants then were asked to describe how they show their students respect.

The researchers emphasized that an empathic mindset toward discipline does not mean being overly permissive. Teachers do have to maintain discipline. They are, however, encouraged to do so in a context of mutual understanding and trust.

At the same time that one group of teachers was receiving empathy training, another group of teachers (the "control group") received similarly structured training in the uses of technology in education. At the end of the school year, the number of student suspensions for each group was compared. The results indicated that students of the teachers who had *not* received empathy training were *twice as likely* to be suspended as students of teachers who had received the training.

Teachers who utilize an empathic approach to discipline are less likely to utilize suspension as a way to deal with student misbehavior. Since empathy decreases stereotypes and prejudice, they are also less likely to discriminate on the basis of race. Students who observe this behavior internalize the teacher's commitment to racial equality.

2) Developing Intergroup Friendships
Students not only observe how teachers behave in the classroom, they also observe their behavior outside of class—in the hallways, in the lunchroom, on the playground, before and after school. When teachers interact in warm, friendly ways with other teachers whose racial background is different from their own, they are providing a bridge-building model for their students. If the teachers can cross the racial divide there is a greater likelihood that their students will do so as well. Similarly, students observe when teachers interact with administrators and other school employees (janitors, lunchroom workers, etc.), and they are influenced by the degree of comfort or discomfort, respect or dismissiveness evidenced across racial lines.

Reading or Listening to Counter-Stereotypical Stories

Stories are a powerful means for influencing attitudes and beliefs. Reading or listening to positive stories about people from a racial group different from one's own has been shown to be an effective activity for reducing children's implicit bias against those of a different group, especially for older children. In one illustrative study (Gonzalez, Steele, & Baron, 2017) three hundred and sixty-nine children of Caucasian and Asian ethnicity between the ages of five and twelve listened to four positive vignettes about an adult man or woman. For one group of children, each vignette was accompanied by a picture of a White man or woman; for a second group, the pictures were of a Black man or woman. A control group listened to stories about four types of flowers. After hearing the stories, all of the children took a well-established test of implicit racial bias. The results of the testing showed that the older children (8 to 12) who heard positive stories about Black people expressed significantly less implicit racial bias than did those who heard either positive stories about White people or stories about flowers. The younger children did not show this difference. The researchers postulated that because of developmental changes, different activities might be needed in order to influence the implicit racial biases of younger children.

Watching Pro-Social Television Shows

Television shows with prosocial, antibias messages are another important avenue for reducing stereotypes and prejudice. For many years, *Sesame Street* has made a consistent effort to expose children to positive messages about diversity. Many studies have found that when children regularly watch this show, they develop more positive attitudes about people from racial and ethnic backgrounds different from their own (Mares & Pan, 2013). In one illustrative example, *Sesame Street* developed a program for Israeli and Palestinian children that showed children from each group being friends with children from the other group. Researchers found that after watching this program, both Israeli and Palestinian children were more open to the possibility of being friends with someone from the other group. They also were more likely to say that it would be wrong to exclude members of the other group from their circle of friends (Brenick, et al., 2007).

Watching shows like Sesame Street provides children with valuable experiences of vicarious positive contact across racial and ethnic lines. These experiences are worthwhile in themselves, but they also provide valuable opportunities for positive discussions with parents and teachers.

Discussions

Most adults, particularly Caucasian adults, have a difficult time discussing racial issues with children. They avoid such discussions because they are afraid that if they bring up the subject of race they won't know what to say. They express concern that they might say the "wrong thing." Adults are often concerned that if they talk with children about race they may be "putting ideas into their heads" that otherwise might not be there.

Research tells us that just the opposite is the case. By age 3, many children have already formed racial stereotypes and prejudicial attitudes (Van Ausdale & Feagin, 2001). Children also frequently develop erroneous ideas about race. For example, in a study conducted before the election of Barack Obama to the U.S. presidency (Bigler, Arthur, Hughes, & Patterson, 2008), children ages 5 to 10 were asked why they thought all U.S. presidents to that point had been White. One-quarter of the children answered that it was illegal for a Black person to become president.

Discussions with adults can help children reduce racial stereotypes and prejudice and correct erroneous beliefs. In the following sections we present research studies and recommendations for helping parents and teachers have productive discussions with children about race.

Parent-Child Discussions

When parents are able to overcome their anxiety and engage in discussions of racial issues with their child(ren), positive things can happen. In a study of the effects of parent-child discussions on children's racial attitudes (Vittrup & Holden, 2010), White parents and their young children (5 to 7 years old) were randomly assigned to either a "discussion group" or a "no discussion" group. The parents in the "discussion group" were asked to engage their child in a race-related discussion each night for five nights in a row. The suggested topics for these discussions included: How children of different racial groups can be great friends and have a lot in common; The importance of showing respect for people regardless of skin color; Asking the child about cross-racial friendships (real or hypothetical) in the neighborhood or at school; and Pointing out that children of each race, ethnicity, and skin color are all special. The comparison group of parents and children (the "no discussion" group) did not have race-related discussions.

At the beginning and end of the study the children took a test that measures racial attitudes and beliefs. The results of the testing showed that the children whose parents had discussed racial issues with them had made significantly more positive changes in their attitudes toward Black people than did those who did not participate in race-related discussions. Talking about race in a positive way had reduced negative stereotypes and increased positive feelings about people with a different skin color.

How should parents talk to their children about race? Many guidelines have been recommended. We believe the following ones have particular merit:

1) Affirm children's questions or comments about race (Feris & Riddick, 2018). For example: "I'm so glad you asked that question" or "I'm so glad you said that." Affirming children's questions and comments communicates an important message—race is not a taboo subject, it's OK to ask questions or make comments about race. Psychologist Earl Grollman, in commenting about challenging subjects, said: "Whatever is mentionable is manageable." If we can talk about issues we can begin to work toward solutions.

   When a child asks a question or makes a comment that reveals a stereotyped belief or a prejudicial attitude, it is critical that parents avoid scolding or shaming the child. Such a reaction shuts down communication, eliminates the opportunity to correct or modify false impressions, and inhibits future conversations on racial topics. Affirmation and reinforcement are important in this context as well—"I'm so glad you asked that question, shared that idea, etc. Help me understand why you believe that—here's what I believe."

2) Discuss issues of "fairness" and "unfairness" about race (Feris & Reddick, 2018). For example, when encountering a fiction or nonfiction book in which racial diversity could realistically be represented (e.g., "Elijah's First Day at School," "Biographies of Women Scientists," etc.), but there are no brown or black faces, seize the opportunity for meaningful discussion. Begin with inquiry—"How did you feel about this book?"; "Is there anything missing?"; "Do you think that's fair?"; "Is there anything we could do about it?" Whatever a child's racial or ethnic background, these discussions can bear fruit.

   This kind of opportunity arose for me (S.F.) while volunteering as a tutor in a specialized reading program at a predominantly African-American elementary school. The young student I was working with was balking at completing a workbook page, finally slamming the book shut and crossing her arms defiantly across her chest. When I asked her what was going on, she said: "Nobody looks like me! Nobody in this whole book!" I asked her to tell me how she felt about that and she was quick to add: "I feel left out, like I don't count!" Recognizing her need to be heard, I asked the program director if we might use her telephone to call the publisher of the book. Permission granted, I called the publisher and wound my way through to the head of Marketing and Curriculum Development. I told him that I was working with an African-American student who would like to talk with him about one of his company's books. I then passed the phone to the student, who said: "I don't like your book! Nobody looks like me! I'm not in any of your stories...my friends neither!" The voice at the other end of the phone responded: "I'm sorry. I hear you. I'll talk with the other people in our company and we'll try to do better." The student replied: "OK then...please do that. Goodbye." She passed the phone back to me and, arms unfolded, head held high, marched back to her desk.

3) Discuss stories that have racial content. For example: *The Other Side* (Woodson & Lewis, 2001) is a moving story about two young girls, one White and one Black, who live next door to each other in the segregated South. Their back yards are separated by a fence; the fence is an important symbol of racial segregation in their community. It becomes clear that the girls want to play together, but they are not allowed to cross over the fence. As the story progresses, they resolve this dilemma by sitting together on the fence and using the "barrier" as their home base. Recognizing the determination and creativity of the children, parts of the world around them begin to shift and the girls are allowed to play together on "the other side."

After reading this story, parent and child can discuss such questions as: "How do you feel about the fence and the rule not to cross over?"; "Do you think having a fence like that is a good idea?" "What do you think about the girls' plan to sit together on the fence?"

4) Be on the lookout for teachable moments. For example, Dr. Beverly Tatum, author of the book "Can We Talk About Race?" (Tatum, 2007), recounts this story: "I was cooking with my 3 year old. We used the last white egg in the carton and then took out another carton, this time brown eggs. My son noted that the eggs were different in color. 'Yes, I said as we cracked both eggs open. But look, they are the same inside. Just like people they come in different shades, but they are the same on the inside." (Emmons, 2018). When we develop positive "race consciousness," we encounter numerous opportunities to pass on our values to the next generation.

Classroom Discussions

As with parents, teachers are often uncomfortable discussing race. Many avoid the subject altogether. That is unfortunate, because research studies (Aboud & Levy, 2000; Aboud & Fenwick, 1999) have demonstrated that constructive classroom discussions about race can be effective means for reducing racial stereotypes and prejudice.

Guidelines for such discussions have been published by Teaching Tolerance, a program of the Southern Poverty Law Center whose mission is to help parents and teachers find constructive ways to help prevent or reduce stereotypes and prejudice. The guidelines for classroom discussions of race provide helpful information for teachers who want to explore racial issues with their students but are unsure about how to proceed (www.tolerance.org).

The initial recommendations are designed to help teachers prepare themselves to initiate and moderate discussions about race. The first suggestion is: "Consider the following statements and select the one that best describes how you feel."

I would rather not talk about race
I am very uncomfortable talking about race
I am usually uncomfortable talking about race

I am sometimes uncomfortable talking about race
I am usually comfortable talking about race
I am very comfortable talking about race

This exercise helps teachers gain a clearer understanding of their own emotional reactions to discussions about race.

The next suggestion is designed to help teachers deepen their understanding by using the following sentence stem activity:

The hard part of talking about race is...
The beneficial part of talking about race is...

As they work on completing these stems, teachers gain greater access to their thoughts and feelings about racial discussions. Their increased understanding can then be applied to the process of initiating and moderating such discussions. Self-awareness is critical for effective facilitation. If teachers are unaware of their own discomfort and their implicit biases and stereotypes, the questions they pose, the content they introduce, and the interpretations they make can be problematic.

After these "getting prepared" steps, the Teaching Tolerance guidelines recommend that teachers develop rules for "creating a safe space." Suggested rules include: "Put downs of any kind are never OK," and "Try to understand what someone is saying before rushing to judgment." We would add two additional rules: "Express your feelings honestly, but with the understanding that other people may feel differently"; and "Be open to learning from other people's experience."

Within the context of a safe space, teachers are urged to carefully monitor the emotional climate during the discussion and respond accordingly: "If the tension in the room appears to be prompting dialogue and learning, continue to monitor but let the conversation play out. If the tension boils over into confrontation that jeopardizes student safety (emotional or otherwise), take steps to diffuse the situation."

I (L.F.) was able to implement the last guideline while facilitating a discussion with a multiracial group of 3rd grade students who were participating in the Calling All Colors program. The lesson that day had been about variations in the melanin content of different people's skin. In the discussion that followed, I asked the group: "What have you heard about people with skin color different from your own?" After a brief moment of reflection, one of the African-American children said: "I heard that White people smell bad." A European-American child responded with: "I heard that Black people are stupid." In rapid succession, many of the children shared stories they had heard about what people of a different race were like. After a while, the emotional temperature in the room began to rise. Both White and Black children were beginning to get angry at what they were hearing about people who looked like them.

At that point I stepped in and clarified my initial instruction: "Please remember that what I asked you to think about was what you have *heard*, not what you necessarily *believe*." Making the question "a step removed" allowed the children to feel less threatened and more like reporters of the world around them.

I then asked the children what they thought about the things they had heard about people from a different racial group. Did they believe those things? The children were quick to assure me that they did not believe the negative stereotypes they had heard. Many of them cited their Calling All Colors experience as the main reason they did not believe the stereotypes. They commented: "Charles is Black and he's not stupid"; "Maria is White and she doesn't smell bad." I then asked: "What do you think you might say to someone telling you bad things about people with a different skin color?" The children immediately came up with a number of excellent responses. For example: "Please don't say things like that, it isn't nice"; or "That is not true"; or "My friend Bill is Black and he's very smart." Engaging the children in active problem solving diminishes feelings of powerlessness and stimulates a sense that "We can change the situation."

Teaching Tolerance recommends a number of steps that older students (grades 6 to 12) can take in order to help them participate productively in difficult discussions. The first step is to "restate what you heard." This step slows down the process and gives the student an opportunity to correct misunderstandings and miscommunications. It also gives the "speaker" an opportunity to experience the "listener" as someone who has cared enough to make a conscientious effort to "take in" what was said.

The second step continues the "slow down" process by asking the students to "count to 10" before responding. This gives the students time to think about their responses and moves them away from immediate emotional responses that may have the potential to derail the conversation.

The third step involves taking a few breaths before responding, which allows students to take the edge off of their emotional reactions and to think about what the other person is saying before generating a response. This also allows the speaker a few seconds to amend or revise their words upon brief reflection.

The fourth step is to "speak with compassion and thoughtfulness." Students are urged to assume that the other participants in the discussion have good intentions and to make a strong effort to understand their point of view. When there is a disagreement about something someone has said, the students are urged to "challenge the statement rather than the person who said it." It is also helpful to ask the students to use "I" language ("I feel" or "I think") rather than accusatory "you" language.

By preparing themselves, creating a safe space, giving students tools to help them during difficult discussions, carefully monitoring the emotional tone of the group, and intervening when needed, teachers can facilitate powerful discussions about race in their classrooms. Such discussions can make a significant contribution to reducing the development of stereotypes and prejudice in children and adolescents.

Cooperative Learning

Cooperative learning is an approach to education that emphasizes the benefits of students working together to solve shared problems or complete shared tasks (Gillies, 2016). Each student is assigned part of the task, and all parts must be completed in order for the group to finish the task. Students collaborate to help everyone understand each part of the task and how they fit together. They encourage and support each other's efforts. Teachers facilitate group interactions by teaching principles for constructive group collaboration, monitoring the group's discussions, encouraging active participation by all group members, asking probing questions, and holding each group member individually accountable for their contributions to the group process.

When cooperative learning groups include a mix of students from different racial/ethnic backgrounds, they have been shown to be an effective way to reduce stereotypes and prejudice (Slavin & Cooper, 1999; Kagan, 2006; Satyaprakasha, 2015). Students who work together in a well-functioning multiracial cooperative learning group experience a decrease in negative reactions to people from racial groups different from their own and an increase in friendships that cross racial lines.

Multicultural and Anti-Bias Education

Multicultural and Antibias education is a unique approach to education based on principles and methodology that support respecting and embracing differences and acting against bias and unfairness (www. Teaching for Change.org). A number of interventions have been developed to help students achieve these objectives. In this section we describe some of those interventions.

Multicultural Curriculum

In a multicultural curriculum, diverse racial and ethnic perspectives are represented. This diversity is evident in the books that students read, the videos they watch, the topics they discuss, and the pictures on the classroom and hallway walls. History lessons include many different groups in many different countries. Current events are discussed from multiple points of view. Through exposure to positive images of individuals and cultures different from their own, students can begin to develop "intercultural competence," the ability to interact effectively with members of different cultures. By representing multiple cultures, educators promote visibility and give a clear message that "everybody counts." As they do so, stereotypes and prejudice are reduced (Johnson & Johnson, 2002).

Teaching About Historical Racism

Teaching about historical racism has been shown to have positive effects on children's attitudes and feelings about race. For example, one study (Hughes, Bigler, & Levy, 2007) showed that European-American children who learned about historical racism held more positive and less negative attitudes toward African-Americans. They also showed an increase in the degree to which they valued racial fairness. Learning about past injustice is a valuable way to help children develop attitudes and beliefs that can play a role in preventing future injustice. Introducing the topic to children as part of their general education leads to greater acceptance of painful reality and less of the denial and defensiveness commonly seen among adults.

Empathy Building

Empathy, the ability to vicariously experience the emotions of another person, is a critical part of positive social interactions. Research studies have demonstrated that providing children with empathy-building experiences is a helpful way to reduce stereotypes and prejudice (Aboud & Levy, 2000; Aboud et al., 2012).

Often role-play is used to help students enhance their emotional understanding of what it's like to "walk in another person's shoes." One well-known example of this type of role play exercise is Jane Elliot's classic "blue eyes-brown eyes" simulation with a class of White third-grade students (Peters, 1970). In Elliot's exercise, on one day all the blue-eyed students were treated in a discriminatory way. The next day all the brown-eyed students were discriminated against. Through participating in this exercise, the students were able to increase their empathic understanding of what it's like to experience discrimination.

In another study (Breckheimer & Nelson, 1976), a mixed-race group of high school students role-played student prejudice and discrimination for six group sessions over a period of three weeks. At the end of this experience, the participating students demonstrated a decrease in racial prejudice and an increased desire to interact with members of a different race.

Building Social-Cognitive Skills

Interventions to strengthen social-cognitive skills are designed to help students learn and practice cognitive skills that have been shown to reduce prejudice (Aboud & Levy, 2000). One such skill is the ability to perceive members of a particular group as multifaceted individuals, not just as members of a group. In one classic study (Katz & Zalk, 1978), 2nd and 4th grade white students were shown pictures of African-American individuals. One group of children learned specific names for each person who was pictured. The other group looked at the pictures but did not learn names for those pictured. Both groups were evaluated for racial prejudice at the end of the experiment and two weeks later. Those children who had learned a name for each of the pictured individuals demonstrated less prejudice than those who did not learn names. Learning someone's name is an important way to individualize that person, rather than just seeing him or her as a member of a racial group.

Another group of investigators (Aboud & Fenwick, 1999) expanded this line of research by evaluating an 11-week curriculum unit for White fifth graders designed to improve the students' ability to process information about individual rather than racial attributes. Through a series of entertaining exercises, students in the experimental group were required to learn a variety of internal attributes (likes, dislikes, interests, etc.) of 30 pictured students from a multiracial class. Students in the control group looked at the pictures but were not required to learn any internal attributes of the pictured students. The results showed that students in the group that had learned about the internal attributes of the people in the pictures, and who were found to have a high degree of prejudice in the pre-test, showed significantly less prejudice when evaluated two months after the intervention. Learning about the specific internal attributes of the pictured children had allowed the students in the experimental group to reduce their level of racial prejudice.

Racially Integrated Schools

In 1970, white students made up roughly 80% of the public school population (Siegel-Hawley, 2012). Today, that percentage is less than 50% (www.nces.gov). These percentages are reflections of the changing demographics of the United States, which is rapidly becoming a majority-minority country.

Despite the fact that White students are now a minority of the total public school population, most White children attend schools in which the majority of the students are White. Most Black and Hispanic children attend schools in which the majority of students are Black or Hispanic. More than 65 years after the Supreme Court's 1952 Brown vs Board of Education decision that repealed the so-called "separate but equal" policy, U.S. schools continue to be highly segregated by race (Nazaryan, 2018).

Racial integration of public schools has been proven to have positive results for all students. Research studies have demonstrated that students who attend racially diverse schools benefit in a large number of ways:

- More productive classroom discussions (Siegel-Hawley, 2012)
- More creative and effective problem-solving skills (Page, 2007)
- Greater understanding of different points of view (Orfield & Frankenberg, 2011)
- Better preparation to work in racially diverse workplaces (Kurlaender & Yun, 2005)
- Reduced racial stereotyping and prejudice (Killen, Crystal, & Ruck, 2007)
- More frequent and more stable friendships with a diverse group of people (Hallihan & Smith, 1985; Wright, Aron, McLaughlin-Volpe, & Ropp, 1997)
- Greater development of *Cultural Competence*, the ability to work with and relate to others across racial and ethnic lines (Garda, 2011)
- Greater likelihood to seek out racially diverse colleges, work environments, and neighborhoods (Perry, 2002)
- Greater sense of civic engagement (Kurlaender & Yun, 2005)

In addition to having a racially diverse student body, schools can benefit by having a racially diverse faculty. Researchers have identified three major hypotheses to explain how racially diverse faculties could be beneficial for minority students (Egalite & Kisida, 2016).

The first hypothesis is that racial minority students would benefit from having role models who look like them in positions of authority. By identifying with these role models, students would be more likely to increase the cultural value they place on academic achievement and reduce their fear of being perceived as "acting White" if they pursue academic success.

The second hypothesis is that teachers of color would be more likely to feel a responsibility to cultivate the potential of students of color. As a result they would be more likely to provide mentorship and insist on the students' best effort on all assignments.

The third hypothesis posits that diverse faculty members would be less likely to stereotype students of color. They would also be more likely to develop culturally relevant curricula and to introduce topics from a perspective that minority students could relate to.

Egalite and Kisida (2016) present research data that support each of these hypotheses. They found that minority students with minority teachers more often report that their teacher "pushes them to work hard, requires them to explain their answers, not to give up when the work gets hard, and accepts nothing less than their full effort." Minority students also reported that their demographically similar teachers "notice if they don't understand a topic and explain it another way." The teachers also "take the time to provide feedback on students' written work so they can understand how to do better in the future."

The researchers acknowledge that having a similar demographic does not always translate into more effective teaching. They do suggest, however, that increasing the diversity of the teacher workforce would increase the potential for a common cultural understanding between minority students and their teachers and that this shared understanding would translate into increased academic achievement.

We believe that White students would also benefit from a racially diverse faculty. Learning from teachers whose racial background is different from their own is likely to increase their cultural competence, decrease their conscious and unconscious stereotypes about people of color, and open their eyes to different ways of understanding the world. The students' perceptions of other people and other cultures would be broadened and deepened.

Diversity Initiatives for Racially Segregated Schools and Communities

Unfortunately, most schools and most communities are not racially diverse. Segregation continues to be the norm. In order for children and adolescents in these communities to experience racial diversity there need to be planned initiatives designed to bring them together in positive ways. In Chapter 2 we described two such initiatives—Calling All Colors and The All God's Children Community Choir. There are many variations on this theme: shared field trips, regular visits between schools, racially diverse dance groups, drama clubs, sports teams, etc. Each of these initiatives shares many of the characteristics of racially diverse cooperative learning groups.

As with all intergroup contact experiences, such initiatives work best when they are organized around the principles of Intergroup Contact Theory: Personal Acquaintance, Equal Status, Cooperative Pursuit of Shared Goals, and Support from Relevant Authorities. In the next chapter we discuss how these principles can be most effectively applied to the types of bridge-building initiatives we have presented in Chapters 2 and 3.

References

Aboud, F. E., & Fenwick, V. (1999). Exploring and evaluating school-based interventions to reduce prejudice. *Journal of Social Issues, 55*(4) 767–785.

Aboud, F. E., & Levy, S. R. (2000). Interventions to reduce prejudice and discrimination in children and adolescents. In S. Oskamp, (Ed.), *Reducing Prejudice and Discrimination* (pp. 269–294). Mahwah, NJ: Lawrence Erlbaum Associates.

Aboud, F. E., Tredoux, C., Tropp, L. R., Brown, C. S., Niens, U., Noor, N. M., & Una Global Evaluation Group. (2012). Interventions to reduce prejudice and enhance inclusion and respect for ethnic differences in early childhood: A systematic review. *Developmental Review, 32*(4), 307–336.

Bigler, R. S., Arthur, A. E., Hughes, J. M., & Patterson, M. M. (2008). The politics of race and gender: Children's perceptions of discrimination and the U.S. presidency. *Analyses of Social Issues & Public Policy, 8*(1), 83–112.

Breckheimer. S. E., & Nelson, R. O. (1976). Group methods for reducing racial prejudice and discrimination. *Psychological Reports, 39*(3, Pt 2), 1259–1268.

Brenick, A., Lee-Kim, J., Killen, M., Fox, N. A., Raviv, A., & Leavitt, L. A. (2007). Social judgments in Israeli and Arabic children: Findings from media-based intervention projects. In D. Lemish & M. Gotz (Eds.), *Children and media in times of war and conflict.* (pp. 287–308), Cresskill, NJ: Hampton Press.

Degner, J, & Dalege, J. (2013). The apple does not fall far from the tree, or does it? A meta-analysis of parent–child similarity in intergroup attitudes. *Psychological Bulletin, 139*(6), 1270–1304.

Egalite, A. J., & Kisida, B. (2016). School size and student achievement: A longitudinal analysis. *School Effectiveness & School Improvement, 27*(3), 1–12.

Emmons, S. (2018). 5 tips for talking about racism with kids. www.parenting.com

Feris, S., & Riddick, L. T. (2018). Strategies for raising race-conscious children. www.raceconscious.org

Garda, R. (2011). The White interest in school integration. *Florida Law Review, 63,* 605. Brief of 553, 2007.

Gilliam, W. S., Maupin, A. N., Reyes, C. R., Accavitti, M., & Shic, F. (2016, September 28). Do early educators' implicit biases regarding sex and race relate to behavior expectations and recommendations of preschool expulsions and suspensions? *Yale University Child Study Center Research Study Brief.* New Haven CT: Yale University.

Gillies, R. M. (2016). Cooperative learning: Review of research and practice. *Australian Journal of Teacher Education, 41*(3), 39–54.

Gonzalez, A. M., Steele, J. R., & Baron, A., D. (2017). Reducing children's implicit racial bias through exposure to positive out-group exemplars. *Child Development, 88*(1), 123–130.

Hallihan, M., & Smith, S. (1985). The effects of classroom racial composition on students' interracial friendliness. *Social Psychology Quarterly, 48*(1), 3–16.

Hughes, J. M., Bigler, R. S., & Levy, S. R. (2007). Consequences of learning about historical racism among European American and African American children. *Child Development, 78*(6), 1689–1705.

Johnson, D. W., & Johnson, R. T. (2002). *Multicultural education and human relations.* Boston: Allyn & Bacon.

Kagan, S (2006). The power to transform race relations. *Teaching Tolerance Magazine,* Fall, p. 53.

Katz, P. A., & Zalk, S. R. (1978). Modification of children's racial attitude. *Developmental Psychology, 14*(5), 447–461.

Killen, M., Crystal, D., & Ruck, M. (2007). The social developmental benefits of inter-group contact among children and adolescents. In E. Frankenberg & G. Orfield (Eds.), *Lessons in integration: Realizing the promise of racial diversity in American schools* (pp. 57–73). Charlottesville, VA: University of Virginia Press.

Kurlaender, M., & Yun, J. (2005). Fifty years after Brown: New evidence of the impact of school racial composition on student outcomes. *International Journal of Educational Policy, Research, & Practice, 6*(1), 51–78.

Mares, M.-L., & Pan, Z. (2013). Effects of *Sesame* Street: A meta-analysis of children's learning in 15 countries. *Journal of Applied Developmental Psychology, 34*(3), 140–151.

Morewedge, C. K, Yoon, H., Scopelliti, I., Symborski, C. W., Korris, J. H., & Kassam, K. S. (2015). Debiasing decisions: Improved decision making with a single train-ing intervention. *Policy Insights from the Behavioral and Brain Sciences, 2*(1), 129–140

Nazaryan, A. (2018). School segregation in America is as bad today as it was in the 1960s. www.newsweek.com, March 22.

Okanoufa, J. A., Paunesku, D., & Walton, G. M. (2016). Brief intervention to encourage empathic discipline cuts suspension rates in half among adolescents. *Proceedings of the National Academy of Sciences, 113*(19), 5221–5226.

Orfield, G., & Frankenberg, E. (2011, January 27). *Experiencing integration in Louisville: How parents and students see the gains and challenges.* Civil Rights Project. University of California, Los Angeles, CA.

Page, S. E. (2007). *The difference: How the power of diversity creates better groups, firms, schools, and societies.* Princeton, NJ: Princeton University Press.

Pahlke, E., Bigler, R. S., & Suizzo, M.-A. (2012). Relations between colorblind socializa-tion and children's racial bias: Evidence from European American mothers and their preschool children. *Child Development, 83*(4), 1164–1179.

Perry, P. (2002). *Shades of White: White kids and racial identities in high school.* Durham, NC: Duke University Press.

Peters, W. (Director). (1970). *The eye of the storm* [TV movie]. American Broadcasting Company.

Satyaprakasha, C. V. (2015). Research studies on effect of cooperative learning on social relations. *International Journal of Education and Psychological Research, 4*(1), 39–45.

Siegel-Hawley, G. (2012). How non-minority students also benefit from racially diverse schools. *Research Brief #8,* National Coalition on School Diverstiy. Retrieved from https://www.school-diversity.org/pdf/DiversityResearchBriefNo8.pdf

Slavin, R. E., & Cooper, R. (1999). Improving intergroup relations: Lessons learned from cooperative learning programs. *Journal of Social Issues, 55*(4), 647–663

Suttie, J (2016). Four ways teachers can reduce implicit bias. *Greater Good Magazine.* www.greatergood.berkeley.edu

Tatum, B. D. (2007). *Can we talk about race?* Boston, MA: Beacon Press.

Todd, A. R., Bodenhausen, G. V., & Galinsky, A. D. (2012). Perspective taking combats the denial of intergroup discrimination. *Journal of Experimental Social Psychology, 48*(3), 738–745.

U.S. Dept. of Education. (2014). Date snapshot: school discipline. *Issue Brief No. 1*, OCR-data.ed.gov

Van Ausdale, D., & Feagin, J. R. (2001). *The first R: How children learn race and racism.* Lanham, MD: Rowman & Littlefield.

Vittrup, B., & Holden, G. W. (2010). Exploring the impact of educational television and parent–child discussions on children's racial attitudes. *Analyses of Social Issues & Public Policy, 10*(1), 192–214.

Woodson, J., & Lewis, E. B. (2001). *The other side.* New York: Putnam.

Wright, S. C., Aron, A., McLaughlin-Volpe, T., & Ropp, S. A. (1997). The extended contact effect: Knowledge of cross-group friendships and prejudice. *Journal of Personality and Social Psychology, 73*(1), 73–90.

www.nces.ed.gov (2017). National Center for Education Statistics, May, 2017.

www.teachingforchange.org. Anti-bias education. *Teaching Social Justice Starting in the Classroom.*

www.tolerance.org. *Let's talk! Discussing race, racism and other difficult topics with students.*

Chapter 4

Intergroup Contact Conditions in Youth, Family, and School Initiatives

Personal contact between individuals from different groups is the most powerful way to reduce stereotypes and prejudice and increase understanding and trust (Pettigrew & Tropp, 2006). However, as described in Chapter 1, not just any contact will do. Psychologist Gordon Allport taught us that intergroup contact is most likely to produce positive change when some or all of certain conditions are present (Allport, 1954). In this chapter we review these conditions and illustrate each one with examples drawn from one or more of the programs and activities introduced in earlier chapters.

Contact Conditions

Personal Acquaintance

In order for positive change to occur, individuals from different racial backgrounds need to interact in personal ways. They need to spend time together, learn each other's names, and talk about their interests and life experiences. People need to know each other as individuals, not mere stereotypes. Just sharing the same space is not sufficient; authentic relationships require positive interactions.

Diversity initiatives can facilitate personal contact by creating opportunities for small group or one-on-one interaction; by creating personal links between individuals with similar interests or circumstances; and by establishing an atmosphere that is warm, open, accepting, and friendly.

All God's Children Choir

In designing the structure for the All God's Children Choir, we were conscious of the need to build in time and opportunities for more personal interactions for choir members and their families. We wanted children and parents to be participants in a process that creates greater familiarity. We did not want the focus to be exclusively on the identified task (rehearsing and performing), with few opportunities for less structured contact. We did not want this to be an activity in which family members passed each other in the "pick up lane" or just poured punch at a postconcert party. We wanted to offer the kind of consistent exposure in shared pursuits that, over time, cultivates meaningful relationships.

At the beginning of each choir rehearsal, five to ten minutes of "gathering time" provide an opportunity for choir members, parents, and directors to exchange greetings, briefly catch up on important events since the last practice, and create name tags, which everyone wears for the entire rehearsal. The name tags allow new members to learn everyone's name, and they serve as helpful reminders for those who have been in the choir for a while. Learning people's names is an important part of developing personal connections. The name becomes an anchor to which other aspects unique to that individual become attached. For example: "Who is Artemisia?"…"She's that smart girl who was the first one to learn the words to the new song, and she's Ashonti's really good friend"; "Who is CJ? … He's the athlete who wore his football jersey to choir practice!…" ;"Who is Antonia?… She's the little girl from Columbia who helped the Directors pronounce the Spanish words for Somos El Barco!"

Many personal interactions occur when the practicing is complete and choir members and families make announcements of happenings in their lives, share a meal, and celebrate birthdays. As parents and grandparents work together to prepare and serve the meal they often discover common interests and areas of concern. Initially, such conversations tend to be about topics like food preferences, allergies, etc., but over time more intimate aspects of life are shared—illness of an aging relative, job frustrations, etc. In this less-structured time, children and teens also talk with one another, compare photos on cell phones, joke and laugh together. Younger choir members are often up and about engaging in a spontaneous game of tag or hide and seek. As they finish eating, teens sometimes gather around the piano to create their own music. The atmosphere is relaxed, informal and collaborative. In many ways, it feels like an extended family gathering.

Choir leaders, aware of special interests or circumstances that children or families have in common, often use that information to facilitate the development of personal connections. For example: "Catherine's family is also new to this area, they moved here about the same time as your family did"; "Jaden just signed up for rocket football, are you playing again this year?"; "Liz, did you know that Krista also home schools her children?" Such links make it easier for children and adults to begin sharing on a more personal level.

A poignant example of how intergroup contact can facilitate personal connection unfolded one summer day as the members of the choir were getting ready to take the stage for a performance at a local band shell. Two of the younger boys in the choir—one Black, one White—were chatting away in the wings of the band shell, waiting to walk onstage with the other members of the group. One of the directors quietly signaled them to stop talking—"the microphones are on!" she said. The boys leaned forward, nose to nose, and continued their conversation, now in a whisper. From the corner of his eye, the White child took note of the tight ebony curls that framed the face of his friend. He reached out, gently placing his palm on the other boy's cheek, and explored the feel of hair quite different from his own. The Black child continued his story without missing a beat, but in response he too extended a hand and tenderly placed his palm along the cheek of his friend. His fingertips ran through the fine, straight locks, and both boys began to smile. They stood this way, facing one another, opposite arms extended, hands resting along the side of each small face—until the choir directors called out, urging them onto the stage. It was just a moment in time, but in its uncomplicated ease, untainted curiosity, and tender expression of trust, the moment spoke volumes about the journey of the All God's Children Community Choir.

Cooperative Learning Groups

When racially diverse students learn together in properly structured cooperative learning groups, stereotypes and prejudice can be effectively reduced. The first structural consideration is the size of the group. Psychologists David and Roger Johnson, who have conducted extensive research on cooperative learning groups, strongly recommend making the group size as small as possible (Johnson & Johnson, 2002). Initially, when students are first learning how to interact in a cooperative learning group, the ideal size is two. As students become more proficient, the group size can be increased, but not by much. The largest recommended group size is four.

The smaller the group, the more opportunities there are for personal interactions. In a group of two to four, students have many opportunities to share their ideas and react to the expressed ideas of the other student(s). These interactions have the potential to promote mutual understanding and trust and decrease stereotypes and prejudice. In a larger group, there are fewer opportunities for personal interactions and more opportunities for one or more students to avoid personal contact with the other group members.

Another important factor in promoting personal interactions in cooperative learning groups is the nature of the task that the group is asked to complete. A number of studies (Gillies, 2016) have found that when the task is open-ended and discovery-based, rather than one that requires a narrow search for the "right answer," students are more likely to communicate with one another and share information in ways that promote the development of positive relationships.

In the initial structuring of cooperative learning groups, and in subsequent monitoring of group process, teachers need to be conscious of the potential impact of prevailing stereotypic beliefs and attitudes. Their teaching behaviors need to maximize the likelihood that this experience will challenge negative stereotypes and foster mutual understanding and respect.

Equal Status

Equal status is an essential condition for fruitful intergroup contact. All groups need to have an equal opportunity to participate in whatever situation they are in. Contact in which there is a status hierarchy is not likely to lead to positive change. This is especially true when that status hierarchy reflects current societal inequities.

Diversity programs can promote equal status by ensuring that individuals from different racial groups are treated with equal regard, that program activities are not culturally biased, that the leadership team is racially diverse, and that the program's location does not favor one group over another.

Calling All Colors

The *Southwest Michigan Calling All Colors* program always begins with a large group educational activity focused on racial diversity. The person facilitating this activity often asks for student volunteers to serve as "assistants." In selecting these volunteers the facilitator deliberately chooses an equal number of students from each of the participating schools.

After the large group activity, the children are divided into smaller groups, with approximately equal numbers of White and Non-White children in each group. Small group leaders make sure that all children have an equal opportunity to participate in every activity. The program selects activities with an awareness of and sensitivity to their meaning for each racial/ethnic group. Care is taken to avoid cultural bias in choice of activity, to make sure that no activities are unfamiliar to one group but commonplace and well-practiced for the other. Participants need the opportunity to get to know each other on a "level playing field."

Calling All Colors also promotes equal status by choosing a "neutral" site for the experience. Neither school is seen as the valued "host" of the program, and inequalities in the physical condition or resources of the two schools do not become the focus of attention.

Cooperative Learning Groups

Equal status is critical to the effective use of cooperative learning groups in breaking down stereotypes and cultivating an appreciation of "the other." Teachers must guard against any societal conditioning that could lead to assigning roles in the groups based on prevailing biases. For example, a White teacher might express unconscious bias by appointing a White student as "coordinator of the group" because "he'll be the most responsible." A Black teacher might express unconscious bias by appointing a Black student as group coordinator because "otherwise the White students won't listen to anything he has to say." Teachers, like all the rest of us, have been influenced by their life experiences and therefore need to be vigilant in situations in which unconscious stereotypical beliefs could affect their attitudes and behaviors with students.

Because students themselves are growing up in families and communities that continue to hold onto stratified notions of the value of different groups, teachers also need to be aware of the tendency of children to spontaneously "award" positions in cooperative learning groups in accordance with those notions. Teachers need to monitor and, if necessary, intervene to interrupt these patterns and ensure more equal status in the group. Ideally, equal status roles emerge naturally as students pool their resources and recognize the value of each members' contribution.

Common Goals and Cooperative Interaction

Personal Acquaintance and Equal Status are important, but often not sufficient to stimulate lasting change. There must also be common goals and cooperative interaction. As noted in Chapter 1, Allport suggested that: "Only the type of contact that leads people to *do* things together is likely to result in changed attitudes…common participation and common interests are more effective than the bare fact of equal-status contact." (Allport, 1954, p. 276).

Cooperative interaction, working together toward a common goal, leads to a sense of interdependence, of each person needing the other (or others) to achieve the shared objective. Such interdependence promotes recognition of the other's strengths, the specific value added by their participation, and therefore is a powerful force for reducing stereotypes and prejudice. As individuals come to know each other, their picture of what "those people are like" begins to change, to become more complex, to become more real.

Diversity initiatives need to establish goals that all participants are enthusiastic about pursuing. The format must provide collaborative experiences that are engaging and meaningful. Activities should be structured so that cooperation and collaboration are seen as essential in achieving the group's goals.

All God's Children Choir

Shared goals and cooperative interaction are essential elements of the *All God's Children Choir*. Working together in a collaborative way is vital for creating harmony in every aspect of the experience.

The children and teens of All God's Children are initially drawn to the choir because they like to sing and look forward to performing before an audience. Many have asked their parents to sign them up after hearing the choir at a special event and taking note of the enthusiasm and camaraderie among choir members. Older children and teens are often attracted to the idealistic themes expressed through the choir's choice of songs, and to the idea of being part of a multiracial/multiethnic group. Common goals, therefore, include: (1) learning and performing a variety of meaningful songs about unity, peace, hope, diversity and inclusion; (2) developing new friendships; (3) having fun; and (4) making a difference by being part of a multiracial, multicultural choir that entertains but also models racial and ethnic harmony for their audiences.

Parents often come with more specific goals in mind—a desire to provide an opportunity for their children, and their family, to participate in a meaningful experience with other children and families whose racial background is different from their own, and a desire to provide a model of the richness of diversity for other families in their community.

During rehearsals, choir members work together to learn new songs, review old ones, and "polish" their repertoire. Special parts are assigned and children and teens collaborate on harmonies and the intricacies of a round. The multiracial, multiethnic team of choir directors takes turns conducting and giving encouragement and constructive feedback to the singers. After practice, families work together to prepare and serve the food and everyone, including the children, participates in clean up.

At performances, the adults help with last-minute preparations—checking that everyone is wearing their choir shirt or vest, taking younger children to the bathroom, making sure all choir members are lined up in the right order prior to taking the stage. Audience feedback often includes admiring comments about the "product" (e.g., "Your songs are so inspiring," "The harmonies were beautiful") but also about the "process" (e.g., "You all seem so comfortable together"; "It seems like an extended family, with everybody pitching in.").

Cooperative Learning Groups

Collaborative interactions in pursuit of shared goals are the core elements of cooperative learning. Students in cooperative learning groups need to agree on their objectives, specify their individual responsibilities, develop a structure and process for achieving their goals, evaluate their progress, and constructively resolve any conflicts that might arise (Gillies, 2016).

In order for cooperative learning groups to lead to positive outcomes, students need to develop and refine a variety of social skills. They need to practice taking turns talking and listening. They need to practice sharing what they have learned and learning from what the other group members have to share. They need to value and affirm the contributions of each group member. They need to discuss any disagreements in a positive, nonaggressive way and work together to reach consensus.

Teachers need to prepare the students by detailing the social skills they will need in order to have a successful group experience. Before the groups begin their work, teachers need to introduce the core concepts of cooperative learning, explaining the value of learning in groups, discussing the structure and process of such groups, and presenting principles for coping with disagreements among group members. Once the groups begin their work, teachers can monitor their progress and intervene when needed to help them move forward in a constructive way. This may include helping them recognize inequities in their process, raising their consciousness about possible roadblocks ahead, and helping them find ways to constructively resolve conflicts between group members.

Teachers need to be aware that racial stereotypes exist in all age groups and that bias may manifest itself in group process. For example, if White students monopolize group discussions and "talk over" Black students' efforts to contribute, the teacher has a responsibility to draw attention to this phenomenon. This intervention must be done in a nonjudgmental, non-shaming way. The teacher may simply call for a pause in the interaction, suggesting: "I'd like for you all to look at the way your conversation is going. Does it seem balanced and fair? Is every participant fully engaged?" The most effective insights will come through the students reflecting on the questions and coming up with their own answers. On rare occasions the teacher may need to identify and explain the problematic pattern. It is important to recognize a "teachable moment" and not be afraid to address the "elephant in the living room."

Repeated Contact Over Time

Repeated contact over time allows for the development of genuine relationships based on actual experiences, rather than limited relationships heavily influenced by stereotypical perceptions and beliefs. With time, a person who was initially seen as "the other" comes to be viewed as a multifaceted individual with whom one shares common interests and concerns. In some instances, he or she may come to be perceived as "my friend."

Diversity programs need to include plans for repeated contacts, structured in such a way that participants are able to have multiple opportunities for personal interaction. Each interaction has the potential to increase understanding and deepen the connection. In addition, continuity over time provides an opportunity for any misunderstandings or misinterpretations to be addressed and resolved.

All God's Children Choir

Repeated contact is an integral part of the *All God's Children Choir* experience. The choir regularly rehearses twice a month. Rehearsals are increased to once a week a few weeks prior to performances, which take place 6 to 8 times a year. Many children, and their families, have participated in *All God's Children* for a number of years—in some instances, beginning at age 4 and continuing through age 18. The frequency and the duration of contact, as well as the meaningfulness of the activity, often lead to deep and significant relationships. Former choir members are seen together in later photos of racially integrated wedding parties, baby showers, super bowl parties, etc. The enduring aspect of these attachments demonstrates that continuity of contact can have lasting impact.

Calling All Colors

Participants in *Calling All Colors* also have repeated contacts, though more limited in time and scope. The students come together for diversity education experiences twice each school year. Their teachers expand on these experiences by arranging pen pal and e-mail exchanges and, on occasion, classroom visits. At the end of the school year students and their families come together for an afternoon of fun, food, and fellowship at the annual Calling All Colors picnic.

During their elementary school years, students participate in Calling All Colors at four different grade levels: first, second, third, and fourth. By the time they enter middle school, they have had many contacts with children from a racial background different from their own, and many opportunities to develop friendships across racial lines. By offering repeated contacts over time, the program avoids the possibility that a single positive experience will be interpreted as an aberration, as an exception to stereotyped perceptions of what "those people" are like. Without the Calling All Colors program, most of these children would never have any personal encounters with anyone whose race/ethnicity was different from their own.

Cooperative Learning Groups

Psychologists David and Roger Johnson have identified three major types of cooperative learning groups: Informal groups, Formal groups, and Base groups (Johnson & Johnson, 2002). *Informal Groups* last from a few minutes to one class period and are designed to achieve limited, but important, learning goals—focusing students' attention on the material to be learned, setting a mood conducive to learning, ensuring that students process and rehearse the material being taught, or providing closure to an instructional session. *Formal Groups* last from one class period to several weeks and are designed to complete a specific project—answering questions at the end of a curriculum unit, designing a survey or experiment, writing a report, etc. *Base Groups* are long-term groups with stable membership. They may stay together for one or more years. These groups provide a foundation to help students develop cognitively and socially in healthy ways.

Each type of group makes positive contributions, but *base groups* provide the most opportunities for repeated contact. A well-functioning base group increases the quality and quantity of student learning, reduces stereotypes and prejudice, and improves mutual understanding and respect.

Intergroup Friendship Potential

"Friendship potential" is a particularly important condition for effective intergroup contact (Pettigrew & Tropp, 2006). Many research studies have found that when children develop friendships with members of racial groups different from their own, they are less likely to harbor stereotypes and prejudice as adults, and more likely to develop adult friendships across racial lines. The best way to create an environment conducive to the development of intergroup friendships is by carefully cultivating as many of Allport's contact conditions as possible.

Diversity initiatives can facilitate the development of interracial friendships by creating opportunities for personal interaction, fostering equal status, providing engaging collaborative experiences, and ensuring repeated contact over time. In addition, group leaders can model interracial friendship in their interactions with one another.

The *All God's Children Choir* has stimulated the development of many intergroup friendships—friendships involving children, teens, parents/grandparents, and choir directors. In addition to interactions during rehearsals and performances, some of these friendships have broadened to include play dates, birthday parties, sleepovers, attending concerts and sports events together, and a variety of other shared activities. There are children who met in the choir during the elementary school years, found they had much in common, and developed close friendships that have continued into their young adult years. Four older girls, who playfully referred to themselves as "the Divas," frequently stayed in touch by phone between rehearsals and performances, socialized at each other's homes, and spontaneously performed as a quartet at an area "open mic." Two of the older boys shared a variety of sports activities and on one occasion attended a Super Bowl party together, along with their fathers. When families are celebrating a special event—first communion, graduation, school play, dance recital—other choir families, as well as choir directors, are often on hand to offer support and a round of applause. When some choir families have experienced hard times, others have responded in a variety of caring ways—sending cards, making phone calls, bringing food, etc.

These intergroup friendships are manifest not only among participants of the same age and gender but also, in some cases, across those boundaries. A European-American mother of three older choir boys found herself reaching out to three younger African-American girls in the choir, sharing tickets to the ballet, Disney movies, and a variety of other activities. In these situations children are not only able to experience peers from the "other" group as friends, they also can refine their perception of adults from the other group as "extended family."

Support by Relevant Authorities

Allport recognized that intergroup contact is most likely to produce positive change when it has the support of community authorities— government officials, school administrators, religious leaders, etc. In addition to providing official sanction for the contact, community leaders can be very helpful by facilitating connections with families, recruiting participants, securing funding, contributing to program development, and helping to monitor the effectiveness of the program in achieving its goals.

Organizers of diversity initiatives need to seek the support of community authorities early in the process of planning the initiative. They need to give clear explanations of the program's goals and how these goals will benefit the community. They need to invite these community leaders to share their thoughts, listen carefully, and be open to integrating suggestions or modifications that might enhance the program and increase the authorities' experience as "stakeholders." Once the program is underway, they need to maintain contact, provide information about what's happening in the program, give feedback regarding the program's demonstrated effectiveness, and seek continuing support and validation.

By forming these alliances, leaders of diversity initiatives are able to use the trust and credibility already established by community leaders as a springboard to help launch the initiative: "If my pastor (or principal, coach, etc.) says you're good, you're good."

Calling All Colors has received invaluable support from the participating schools' superintendents, principals, and teachers. From the beginning, most superintendents and principals recognized the importance of diversity education and welcomed the opportunity to collaborate with the Calling All Colors staff in order to provide meaningful contact across racial and ethnic lines. These authorities agreed to provide bus transportation, free of charge, from their schools to the Calling All Colors location, and they encouraged their teachers to sign up and participate in the program. Many teachers have become enthusiastic allies. They have attended training sessions and have expanded the program by facilitating subsequent pen-pal and email exchanges, as well

as occasional visits to one another's classrooms. Their additional reinforcement of concepts introduced during Calling All Colors, through
relevant classroom discussions and links to their own curriculum, has
kept the lessons learned alive and ever expanding.

Modeling

As discussed in Chapter 1, we have found that in diversity programs for
young people, modeling is an important addition to Allport's Contact
Theory conditions. Adult leaders need to demonstrate that they are able
to interact with others from different racial backgrounds in ways that
are equal and respectful. They need to be clear about the value added
through each leader's participation. When there are differences of opinion they need to model positive communication and collaborative problem solving. Adults need to "walk the walk," not just "talk the talk."

In the *All God's Children Choir*, adult modeling is readily apparent in
the easy camaraderie and shared leadership of the multiracial team of
choir directors (two White, three Black) and in the friendly, cooperative
interactions among choir parents and grandparents. In addition, the
members of the choir's Older Group provide a model for the younger
children of comfortable, mutually supportive interactions. In many
ways, older peers are the most likely source of identification for their
younger counterparts. The community benefits as the choir provides a
model of collaboration and personal connections before, during, and
after performances. That impact is further experienced when the choir
is "out and about" attending community events.

In *Calling All Colors*, modeling is provided by the collaborative interactions between Black and White group facilitators and teachers.
The ease they demonstrate across racial lines prepares the children to
leave the opening assembly and enjoy their own interracial contacts
in their small groups. In the community, encounters between children
who have shared the Calling All Colors experience provide a model
of comfortable, spontaneous interaction between children from "both
sides of the river." Stories of chance encounters at a mall, a sports event,
or a movie theater validate our belief that the program's impact can be
felt beyond its "borders."

Effective and Ineffective Contact

When all or most of the "conditions for effective intergroup contact" are present, interactions between individuals from different racial/ethnic groups lead to positive attitudinal and behavioral changes. When they are not present, change is less likely to occur. For example, school integration without the support of teachers and principals, and without careful planning for cooperative interaction, is not likely to lead to significant change. Competition between all-Black and all-White athletic teams is more likely to reinforce stereotypes than it is to reduce them. When interaction is limited to people of color providing services (cleaning, yard work, etc.) to White people, stereotypes are likely to persist. Contact alone is not enough to produce significant change. There must also be personal acquaintance, equal status, common goals, cooperation, repeated contact over time, friendship potential, support by relevant authorities, and modeling.

Indirect Contact

As we noted in Chapter 1, research studies have demonstrated that merely observing positive contact between individuals from different racial groups can stimulate positive attitudinal and behavioral changes in the observer. Such indirect contact is an important means through which diversity initiatives exert their positive effects.

   All God's Children and Calling All Colors both provide the community with many opportunities for indirect contact. The Choir has provided such opportunities to thousands of audience members at their performances, and to those who have observed the children, parents, grandparents, and choir directors when the group has attended a community event or practiced in a community setting (e.g., Art Center, Children's Museum, or Community Room at the mall). Children who have participated together in *Calling All Colors* provide indirect contact experiences for their families and for those who observe their friendly interactions as they occasionally encounter each other in a variety of community settings and at educational experiences shared by multiple schools. One such experience occurred when all fourth grade classes in

Southwest Michigan gathered in the large auditorium of the local community college for an educational enrichment program. As the children entered the auditorium, a high degree of guardedness was evident between classrooms of Black and White students. They looked at each other warily; the atmosphere was tense and, in some cases, hostile. The climate shifted dramatically, however, when two groups of students who had shared the Calling All Colors experience filed into the auditorium from two separate entrances. As the students recognized their "buddies" from Calling All Colors they spontaneously began calling out warm greetings: "Hey, DeShaun, I didn't know you'd be here"; "That's Mary, my Calling All Colors buddy"; etc. Within a few short minutes, a ripple effect became apparent, and the mood in the entire auditorium began to change. These Black and White students were exhibiting a form of interracial interaction—warm, personal, friendly— that is rarely seen in this highly segregated community. As other students observed these interactions they became less tense, less guarded, and more aware of the possibilities for bridging the racial divide.

References

Allport, G. W. (1954). *The nature of prejudice.* Reading, MA: Addison-Wesley.

Gillies, R. M. (2016). Cooperative learning: Review of research and practice. *Australian Journal of Teacher Education, 41*(3), 39–54.

Johnson, D. W., & Johnson, R. T. (2002). *Multicultural education and human relations: Valuing diversity.* Boston, MA: Allyn & Bacon.

Pettigrew, T., & Tropp, L. R. (2006). A meta-analytic test of intergroup contact theory. *Journal of Personality and Social Psychology, 90*(5), 751–783.

Chapter 5

Bridge Building Activities
for College Students

Racial diversity on college and university campuses has been an issue of great interest, and great controversy, for many years. In the 1960s, affirmative action policies emerged from the Civil Rights movement and colleges and universities began to devise ways to increase the racial diversity of their student bodies. In 1978, the U.S. Supreme Court banned the practice of reserving a specific number of spots for racial minorities ("quotas") but allowed colleges and universities to consider race as one factor among many in making admissions decisions (Regents of University of California vs Bakke, 1978). The rationale for this decision was, and continues to be, that diversity on campus enhances learning and prepares students to function more effectively in diverse work settings.

Extensive research has documented the benefits of campus diversity (Wells, Fox, & Cordova-Coba, 2016). These benefits include enhanced student motivation, more engaging classroom discussions, improved critical thinking and problem-solving skills, and increased general knowledge and intellectual self-confidence. Diversity also leads to reduced implicit racial bias, a greater capacity for students to live with and learn from people of diverse backgrounds, and better preparation for employment in work environments that are increasingly diverse.

In this chapter we examine a variety of ways that colleges and universities can facilitate effective diversity on their campuses. We begin with courses that focus on subjects related to these issues, using our course on The Psychology of Stereotypes and Prejudice as a detailed illustration.

Courses on Subjects Related to Diversity

Soon after moving to Southwest Michigan, we created a course at the local community college (Lake Michigan College) on The Psychology of Stereotypes and Prejudice. Our goals were to help students learn about theories and research on these phenomena and to engage them in dialogues, with the two of us and with one another, that would help them gain greater insight into their own feelings and thoughts and a deeper understanding of the impact of differing life experiences.

The major impetus that led us to create this course was our awareness of the large racial divide in our area. We hoped that by helping our students develop a clearer understanding of stereotypes and prejudice, and of the ways that these phenomena had impacted their lives and the lives of others, that a bridge might be built across the racial divide.

We decided at the outset to keep the size of the class small, 20 students or less, in order to create a space in which meaningful dialogue could develop. We wanted the students to know one another as individuals rather than stereotypes. We wanted them to feel safe enough to share their experiences and their genuine thoughts and feelings, and we wanted them to listen carefully to the experiences, thoughts and feelings of their fellow students.

We knew that discussions about race can be difficult. They can be too superficial or too intense. They can become distant and intellectualized or raw and emotionally charged. Finding the right middle ground can present a challenge. Discussions about race can prompt defensiveness and/or withdrawal. Teaching a course that includes such discussions requires self-awareness, as well as knowledge and skill as a facilitator.

Helen Fox, who pioneered teaching about diversity at the University of Michigan, offers good advice in her seminal book "When Race Breaks Out: Conversations About Race and Racism in College Classrooms" (Fox, 2001). Some of her suggestions include: (1) "Use lectures, film, texts, and other formal means of instruction that present various points of view, allowing students to grapple with the material through short papers and other writing activities"; (2) "Start slowly, with positive, safe, egalitarian sharing about identities and cultures. Give students good reasons to want to get to know people from different identity groups"; (3) "Choose readings that move students gradually into the emotions and conflicts...Passionate readings are more valuable after students have learned some facts, definitions, and histories and are more attuned to present-day realities"; (4) "Show understanding and encouragement for angry, exasperated, or frightened students in various stages of their identity development...Reassure students that emotion and conflict over these issues are normal"; and (5) "Model sensitive cross-race/cross cultural interactions...Show how respectful questioning and listening for understanding can further the dialogue."

Our teaching approach closely adheres to Helen Fox's suggestions. We begin by playing a video, "A Place at the Table" (Teaching Tolerance, 2000) that features a group of young adults of different races and ethnicities talking about the history of their people. Much of this history is painful—persecution of American Indians; slavery and Jim Crow; discrimination against Irish immigrants; persecution of Jews during the Holocaust. As these stories are being told, the young adults in the video are very supportive of one another. They stay engaged despite the pain and discomfort. There is no conflict, and by the end of the video they have bonded in a way that is inspiring.

As our students discuss this video, a variety of thoughts and feelings emerge. Some students are shocked by what they have seen and make comments like: "I had no idea that so many terrible things have happened." Other students express surprise that these painful realities "are news to you." Some students say they were aware of many of these painful realities but not aware of others: "I knew about slavery and the Holocaust, but I wasn't aware of the persecution of the Irish immigrants." Some students are defensive: "What does this have to do with what's happening today? I'm not responsible for slavery—I wasn't even born yet when all of this was going on." Some students express appreciation for the opportunity to learn about the history of stereotypes, prejudice and discrimination and about the origins of some of their remnants—emotional, cognitive, socioeconomic—that continue to impact our society today. Some students remain conspicuously silent.

The initial discussion of the video marks the beginning of a process of engaging students in safe dialogue about "taboo" subjects. Over time, our goal is to foster increasing comfort and willingness to risk sharing some of the most difficult thoughts and feelings that the class material is eliciting.

After the initial meeting, the format of the class consists of discussions based on readings and additional videos. The readings review theories and research on stereotypes, prejudice and discrimination. Discussions of these readings initially focus on clarification of concepts and research findings. As the class moves forward, emotionally charged issues begin to emerge. One of the most controversial issues is Affirmative Action. Some White students express strong feelings of resentment about this issue, based on their perception that White people are being discriminated against in college admissions and employment. One student complained bitterly that her mother "lost out" on a job because of Affirmative Action. She insisted that at the present time White people are the most frequent victims of racial discrimination. When other students suggested to her that Affirmative Action was needed because of past and current discrimination against racial minorities she objected strongly: "That was then, this is now—two wrongs don't make a right. I didn't cause the problem so I shouldn't be punished for it." A Black student pointed out to her that while she didn't cause the problem of racial discrimination, she has benefitted from it, and continues to do so in a multitude of ways. The White student was not convinced by this argument, but she didn't reject it out of hand. She agreed to think about it.

This discussion was certainly emotionally charged, but it did not deteriorate into hostile confrontation and personal attacks. Ground rules had been established in the first class meeting and were adhered to. As instructors, we monitored the exchanges and intervened when necessary to keep the conversation meaningful but not explosive. We reflected the students' comments in ways that could lead to a resolution of the conflict: "You're angry because you feel that White people are being treated unfairly. I understand that. But what do you think about the idea that while White people today didn't cause racial discrimination against minority groups, over time we have benefitted from it? I can think of many ways I have benefitted from being White; can you think of some ways that you might have benefitted?" By acknowledging our shared unfair advantage, we were able to help the student lower her guard a bit, and at least consider the possibility that over time she and her mother had benefitted from discrimination against racial minorities.

As the course proceeds, many White students become increasingly open to acknowledging their own racial stereotypes, prejudices, and even some forms of discriminatory behavior. A middle-aged White student tearfully recounted a story that he said he had never shared with anyone, a shame-filled story of an experience he'd had as a young boy in the Southern town where he grew up. His primary caregiver had been a Black "nanny," a warm, nurturing woman whom he "adored." A school friend had invited him over to play, and since their homes were some distance apart the Nanny had offered to give him a ride. As they approached the friend's house, he suddenly bent down, pretending to tie his shoe, so that he wouldn't be seen by his White peers riding in a car with a Black person. Looking up from his lowered stance he saw a tear glistening as it ran down his caregiver's cheek. They were both silent but their eyes met in a telling gaze before he darted from the car. He shared with all of us that "I have felt guilty ever since that day." Even as an eight year old, he was aware of the prejudice that surrounded him and "because I was afraid I'd be rejected I abandoned her, my very best friend...I'm so ashamed."

Not only did this student encourage other White students in the class to reflect on and share their experiences, he also demonstrated genuine remorse and a commitment to "tackle these issues." This revelation had a positive impact on the Black students, who made it clear that in their life experience White people rarely assumed any responsibility for their biased behavior. By the end of the story, the entire class was offering support and urging the White student to use his experience to help make the world a better place.

In the middle of the course, we show a second video, "Skin Deep" (Reid, 1995), in which a group of college students from a variety of racial/ethnic backgrounds meet for a weekend retreat to talk about race relations. Unlike the first video we show, this one contains a significant amount of verbal conflict. The minority students in the group express a great deal of anger about the racial discrimination that they have endured. The White students feel under assault and complain that they are there because they want to make things better but "all we get is anger." Over the course of the weekend the students gradually get to know one another in a more personal way and the initial tension is significantly reduced. The conflicts are not fully resolved, but some important issues are clarified, some insights are gained, and some friendships across racial lines are developed.

We deliberately schedule this more evocative video midway through the course so that the students have had time to develop familiarity with each other and trust in the instructors' ability to maintain a "safe space." When our students discuss this video, intense emotional reactions frequently emerge. Black students often express a lot of anger toward a White student in the video who comes from the South and tries to explain his relatives' racism as "a part of our culture." They are less angry, but still frustrated, with the other White students in the video, who they perceive as defensive and not really listening to the expressed feelings of the minority students. The White students in our class often react the same way as the White students in the video: "This is so unfair—the White students are there because they want things to be better, but the minority students are constantly attacking them." During the course of the discussion, we try to model empathic listening, clear communication, and respectful responding. We also reinforce those behaviors when we observe them in our students. For example: "Jamal, I appreciate your response to Jerry. You were clear about your feelings but you didn't attack him personally"; "Mary, it sounds like you were really listening to Allene and really caring about what she has gone through." Later in the discussion it is often helpful to ask: "What did you learn from the video and the discussion that followed that is helping you to better understand yourself and "the other"? Any new insights? Any new ideas about how you might behave differently going forward?"

Our students' increased tolerance for expressing and hearing strong emotions on racially charged topics is an important byproduct of this process. Over the course of the semester we see less avoidant or attacking behavior and a greater willingness to engage in difficult discussions in mutually respectful, productive ways. Observing, and helping, our students develop this skill set has been very gratifying and encouraging in our efforts to build bridges across the racial divide.

In addition to readings, videos, and discussions, students in our course submit two written assignments. The first assignment is to write a short paper about a movie in which issues related to stereotypes and prejudice are of significance (we supply a list of movie recommendations but we are also open to students' own ideas).

The second written assignment is due near the end of the semester. Students are asked to reflect upon the basic concepts that we have explored and the personal insights that they have developed. They are encouraged to acknowledge a stereotype and/or prejudice they have become aware of harboring and to find and interview someone who seems to fit that stereotype. The goal is for them to have an opportunity to "walk in that person's shoes." Suggested interview questions include: "When was the first time you were aware that you were experiencing prejudice or discrimination, or being seen in a stereotypical way?" "What did that feel like?" "What was the impact of that experience on you and your life?" "How did it affect you moving forward?" "What other experiences of stereotypes, prejudice, or discrimination have you encountered?" "What effect did those experiences have on who you are and where you find yourself today?"

Students not only report these interviews in detail but are also called upon to reflect further on what this interview process meant for them: "How did you feel about what you heard?" "Did it alter your thoughts and feelings?" "In what ways?"

After the papers are submitted, a class discussion allows students to share insights with their classmates. These discussions are helpful ways for students to verbally express what they have learned and to learn from one another. In our experience, the entire process of this interviewing and writing project leads to broadening awareness and understanding and a deepening capacity for empathy. In some instances, a lasting friendship has developed between the student and their interviewee. For example: A White student who came from a highly segregated community had recognized, as the course proceeded, that he had absorbed many of the stereotypes and prejudices toward people of color that were pervasive in his family and in neighboring households. He also recognized that though he had frequent interactions in his workplace with Black coworkers, he knew "nothing about them!" In response to our assignment, he invited one of these "acquaintances" to share a lunch hour and asked if he could talk with him about some of his life experiences. After an hour it became clear that more time would be needed, so a follow up session was set up. Our student not only found himself profoundly moved by his coworker's life experiences, he was also surprised to discover how much he and this Black man had in common. That discovery led to more lunches and a golf outing. A shared experience between equals, collaborating rather than competing, led to the development of an authentic relationship and the weakening of long held stereotypes and prejudice.

Through the writing assignments, students are able to sharpen their understanding of the concepts they are learning by applying them to the lives of individuals, real or fictionalized. They are also able to deepen their understanding of themselves by focusing on their reactions to other people's experiences of being on the receiving end of unfair treatment based on distorted perceptions. Students sometimes recognize themselves as the "victim" or "perpetrator" of discriminatory behavior: "I know just how that woman felt" or "I didn't even realize I did that to people of color."

In the final part of the course, students learn a variety of ways to reduce stereotypes, prejudice, and discrimination. We study Intergroup Contact Theory as well as cognitive and emotional activities that have been shown to effectively decrease these destructive processes. We also explore constructive actions that students can take when they encounter prejudice in others. One student, who was taking our course as part of his theology degree at a nearby university, talked about how conflicted he felt when he returned from holiday celebrations with his extended family. At those gatherings some family members expressed racist ideas and made racist jokes. Fearing conflict or disapproval, our student consistently remained silent. Though he had always been uncomfortable with the expressions of racial prejudice, participation in our class had made silence unbearable. He volunteered, with obvious emotional distress, that "every time I drive away from a family holiday celebration I feel like I have lost a part of my soul." He declared that he was now determined to begin talking with his relatives about their racist remarks. Through class discussions, he gained confidence that he could do this in ways that might be helpful to many members of his family. He recognized that such discussions would not be easy but he felt increasingly confident that he could find ways to make them productive. And perhaps most importantly, he recognized that even if family members clung rigidly to their prejudices and became defensive, even if they were angry with him for making them uncomfortable and challenging the status quo, it was something he needed to do in order to feel "whole," to be a person of integrity.

In addition to the course we teach, we also serve as guest lecturers in other people's courses. On one occasion, we were invited to talk with a group of seminary students at a nearby university about race relations in our area. We presented the results of a survey of racial attitudes and behavior conducted by the two of us and our colleagues on the Race Relations Council of Southwest Michigan (an organization that we will discuss at length in the next chapter). In the question and answer period that followed our presentation, we were startled to hear questions from the White students in the class that basically took the form of: "Weren't problems with race relations solved by the civil rights movement?" We made clear that very significant problems with race relations remain, and that those problems are manifested in many ways right here in Southwest Michigan. Black students jumped in, expressing appreciation for our presentation and describing to their White peers the various ways that racial prejudice and discrimination had impacted their lives and continued to do so to this day. The African-American professor who had invited us described a recent incident in which he was driving his new vehicle and was pulled over by the local police and interrogated about how he got "such a nice car." As teachers and students compared notes on dramatically different life experiences, we could feel a shift in the attitudes of both White and Black students. There was not only the development of a more realistic view of race relations but also a stronger empathic connection between all of the soon-to-be ministers in the room.

Speakers and Panels on Diversity

In addition to courses, colleges can promote diversity by scheduling speakers and panels that address different aspects of this subject. At Lake Michigan College, the Race Relations Council of Southwest Michigan schedules a yearly panel on diversity during the week of Dr. Martin Luther King, Jr's birthday commemoration. Over the years, these panels have addressed a variety of diversity-related issues, including: "Diversity in Education," "Diversity Issues in the Criminal Justice System," and "Strategies for Countering Racial Stereotypes, Prejudice, and Discrimination." Each year, three or four panelists from different racial backgrounds talk about their knowledge and experience related to the particular aspect of diversity that is being highlighted. The audience, composed of students, faculty, administrative staff, and community members, is consistently quite diverse and is actively engaged in the discussion that follows the presentations. The expertise of the presenters and the reactions and life experiences of audience members create a lively and enlightening dialogue. The presence of an experienced facilitator is helpful in monitoring time and tensions to ensure a balanced and fruitful experience. On multiple occasions participants have asked for follow-up sessions in order to continue the dialogue and search for "solutions" to the challenges detailed in the forum.

For individuals with time constraints or those just beginning their own processing of these issues, an opportunity to attend events with knowledgeable speakers or panels can offer a beginning step toward bridging the racial divide. For others such an experience provides an opportunity to forge links to ongoing groups and projects—for example, the Race Relations Council, Calling All Colors, or the All God's Children Choir.

Diversity Training for Students

Because of the increasing significance of diversity and inclusion, many colleges and universities have instituted diversity training programs for their students. One prominent example is the *Freshmen Diversity Experience* at the University of Oklahoma, which has received two Excellence in Diversity Awards from *Insight Into Diversity*, the largest and oldest diversity and inclusion publication in higher education (University of Oklahoma, 2017).

The *Freshmen Diversity Experience* is a research-based program that is a requirement for all incoming first year students. The students can participate in the program either during the summer before they begin taking classes, or during their first academic year. Among the goals of the program are to: (1) "Help students understand stereotypes, and how the resulting prejudice and discrimination can harm groups and individuals, even unintentionally"; (2) "Introduce students to concepts such as implicit bias, stereotype threat, and attributional ambiguity"; (3) "Provide students with the opportunity to practice positive interaction in ways that recognize rather than repress identity issues"; (4) "Introduce students to the many ways they can celebrate cultural diversity"; and (5) "Provide students with effective techniques for active intervention in situations where the values of respect and diversity are being undermined." The methods of instruction used in this program include: "Self-reflective practices"; "Conversations with other students of different identities"; "Perspective taking to build cognitive empathy"; and "Reinforcing a growth mindset for all members of the university community."

Is Diversity Training with College Students Effective?

Many studies have examined the short-term effectiveness of a variety of techniques used in diversity training programs. Most of these have demonstrated some degree of short-term effectiveness in reducing implicit (unconscious) or explicit (conscious) racial bias.

One study (Devine, Forscher, Austin, & Cox, 2012) used a multifaceted training program and assessed longer-term changes (4 to 8 weeks). Participants in the study were 91 non-Black (85% White) students enrolled in an introductory psychology class. Participants were randomly assigned to either a control condition or an intervention condition.

Initially, all students completed the Implicit Association Test (IAT), the most common measure of implicit bias (Greenwald, McGee, & Schwartz, 1998). After the students took the test an experimenter computed their score and asked them to type the score into a computer. The computer provided the students with a report about their score, telling them that they either had a strong, moderate, or slight bias in favor of either Blacks or Whites. As expected, 90% of the participants implicitly favored White people over Black people. The purpose of the feedback was to increase the students' awareness of their implicit bias.

Once they had received their feedback the students in the control condition were dismissed, but were reminded that they would return to the lab two subsequent times and would receive questionnaires to fill out between their lab sessions. Students in the intervention condition were presented with a 45-minute narrated and interactive slide show, separated into education and training sections.

The education section introduced the idea of "prejudice as a habit," as well as how implicit biases develop and are automatically activated without intention. Participants were then taught about the prevalence of implicit race biases and how they can lead people to unwittingly perpetuate discrimination.

The training section introduced students to five strategies for breaking the prejudice habit:

- *Stereotype replacement*—recognizing that a cognitive, emotional, or behavioral response is based on stereotypes; labeling the response as stereotypical; reflecting on why the response occurred; considering how the biased response could be avoided in the future; and replacing the biased response with an unbiased one. A similar process can be applied to societal (e.g., media) stereotyping.
- *Counter-stereotypic imaging*—imagining in detail an individual who is very different (and much more positive) than the stereotype. This might be a made up person, a famous person, or someone the participant knows. By practicing this technique, the positive image can be made available when challenging a stereotypical reaction.
- *Individuation*—obtaining specific information about a member of a stereotyped group. This helps to generate person-specific reactions rather than stereotyped ones.
- *Perspective taking*—actively taking the perspective (empathizing) with individuals from stereotyped groups. This strategy can ameliorate automatic stereotypical reactions.
- *Increasing opportunities for contact*—seeking opportunities to engage in positive, equal status contact with outgroup members. As we have seen, this strategy reduces bias and increases mutual understanding.

Each of these strategies was "explained in straightforward language with concrete examples of everyday situations in which it could be used." The students were then asked to think about situations in their own lives where they could use each strategy. As a unit, the strategies were described as a powerful toolkit for breaking the prejudice habit. The researchers made clear, however, that practice would be required in order for the students to be able to use them effectively. At two and six weeks after the intervention the students completed an open-ended questionnaire in which they were asked whether they had used each strategy and for those they had used to describe one or two situations in which they had used the strategy and to provide general comments about their experiences using that strategy.

Following the intervention the students were reminded to return to the lab for two subsequent sessions and that they would be receiving questionnaires to complete between the lab sessions. They were then dismissed.

In addition to the Implicit Bias Test, the effects of the intervention were assessed with a variety of explicit measures: (1) The Attitudes Toward Blacks scale; (2) Internal and External Motivation to Respond without Prejudice scale; (3) Should and Would scale, which measures the responder's beliefs about how (s)he *should* respond to a particular situation and how (s)he thinks (s)he *would* respond; (4) Concern About Discrimination scale, which measures the degree to which the respondent thinks racial discrimination is a problem.

The results of this study were:

- The Implicit Bias Test scores of the Intervention group were significantly lower than those of the Control group four weeks and eight weeks after the intervention. There was no deterioration in the Intervention group scores from four to eight weeks, indicating a stable reduction in implicit racial bias.
- Intervention group participants had significantly higher concern about discrimination scores and this difference increased between four and eight weeks.
- Students in the intervention group were significantly more aware of how often they would be likely to respond in a biased way than were students in the control group.

To summarize, this study found strong evidence that a multifaceted diversity training program can produce enduring reductions in implicit racial bias, increased concern about racial discrimination, and increased awareness of one's own implicit biases.

In reviewing these findings and the approach that generated them, we would suggest that the efficacy is a result, in part, of avoiding shaming and blaming. By normalizing the "habit" of holding stereotypes and operating with unconscious bias, the program stimulates less defensiveness and resistance and greater openness to change. Diversity training initiatives like this one are important elements in a comprehensive college diversity program.

Diversity Training for Faculty

In order for students to most effectively learn about diversity, faculty members need to recognize their own blind spots and learn how to incorporate diversity into their teaching. Since many faculty members have not developed that expertise, colleges and universities are creating programs to help them acquire the necessary knowledge and skills.

At American University, a Faculty Development Leadership Cohort (FDLC) on Diversity and Inclusion was set up as a vehicle to "train the trainers" (Sangillo, 2018). In October and November, 2017, fourteen racially diverse faculty members participated in five four-hour sessions led by a psychologist who had formerly been the Chief Diversity Officer at a nearby university. The training sessions were focused on helping faculty members "develop their competence, expertise, and understanding" about how to incorporate diversity and inclusion into their teaching. The facilitator introduced a series of questions: "How do you teach in a way that's inclusive? How do you engage students from different backgrounds and cultures and identities? How do you make sure that students see themselves in the syllabus and in the curriculum?"These questions led to intense discussions, in which the faculty members engaged with one another in "processing our own relationship with issues of diversity and race and inclusion." They then moved on to learn about pedagogical tools for teaching diversity and inclusion that they could share with their colleagues.

One important focus of the training was learning how to respond to emotionally charged issues when they emerge in class—a racial incident on campus, an offensive comment during a class discussion, etc. The facilitator shared student surveys indicating that: "When faculty ignore an issue that comes up in the classroom, students from vulnerable groups often read that silence as agreement with what was said."

Faculty members need to intervene at those moments to facilitate discussions that produce positive learning experiences. Diversity training programs provide an opportunity for faculty to develop the knowledge and skills needed for effective intervention.

Once the cohort members had completed their training, they began meeting with other faculty members for 75–90 minute sessions to share what they had learned. Feedback from faculty was generally very positive, especially about the faculty-to-faculty engagement, which one respondent described as "the most meaningful and impactful" aspect of the training experience. That same respondent said: "This was the best training program I have experienced at American University in the 20 years I have been here." These results are quite encouraging and should serve as a prompt to all educational institutions to explore and implement similar training for faculty and staff. Greater self-awareness and added skill in positive intervention can have a powerful impact on all concerned.

Recruiting and Retaining a Racially Diverse Faculty

Colleges and universities often claim that racial diversity is a central value of their institution. The faculty, however, at the majority of these institutions continues to be mostly White. Professor Daryl Smith, who has extensively studied diversity in higher education, suggests that building and maintaining a diverse faculty is essential for creating a truly diverse institution, and that the lack of faculty diversity is becoming "an increasingly urgent issue facing college campuses" (Smith, 2015, p. 147).

Why is faculty diversity important? Based on numerous research studies, Professor Smith offers the following compelling reasons:

- Student advising and mentoring: Students from diverse backgrounds benefit from being able to seek out faculty from similar backgrounds for advising and mentoring
- Career modeling: Diverse faculty create visible models of career possibilities

- Decrease in stereotyping: Having a diverse faculty creates more opportunities for faculty members to be seen as individuals rather than stereotypes.
- Evidence of institutional commitment to diversity: Diversifying the faculty is essential in order for an institution to be seen by prospective students and faculty as committed to diversity
- Developing diverse forms of knowledge: Diverse faculty bring diversity themes to scholarship, increase diversity in the curriculum, and introduce more and different forms of teaching.
- Better institutional decision-making: Faculty from diverse racial and ethnic backgrounds contribute to more fully-informed decisions at all levels of higher educational institutions.
- Attracting and retaining diverse faculty members: A diverse faculty is essential for the creation of a work environment that will be attractive to faculty recruits from diverse backgrounds.

We would suggest an additional reason that a racially diverse faculty is important. When there is diversity, faculty members from different racial groups are able to model positive contact across racial lines. There is an opportunity to demonstrate collaboration, mutual respect, camaraderie, and friendship. When students observe positive intergroup contact by faculty members they are more likely to be open to the possibility of having such contact themselves. For example: when we were invited by our African-American friend to be guest lecturers in his seminary class, the students watched our interactions with their professor very carefully. He greeted us with much enthusiasm and a warm embrace, urging his students to thoughtfully consider our perspective on race relations in Southwest Michigan. During the discussion that followed our lecture, there were several lively exchanges between us, the professor, and the students. In underscoring the value of one another's contributions, it became abundantly clear to the students that these colleagues held one another in high regard. The modeling from our interactions was an important lesson for the students to take away from that class. When educational institutions are lacking in diversity, students miss some of life's critical lessons.

The value of faculty diversity has also been apparent every time the Race Relations Council has presented a forum on race-related topics at Lake Michigan College. The Council's panel is always purposely diverse. We want students, faculty, staff, and community members to experience diversity in action. Each panel member brings a unique perspective to the topic at hand. Their warm, respectful interactions—questions, comments, and validating statements—demonstrate the richness that diversity provides.

Given the importance of faculty diversity, it is striking that college and university faculties are still so predominantly White. Dr. Damon Williams, author of Strategic Diversity Leadership, suggests the following approaches for changing this situation (Williams, 2013):

1) Proactive faculty recruitment policies: College and University administrators need to work with faculty departments and search committees to create proactive strategies for recruitment of diverse faculty members. Just saying in a job description that the institution does not discriminate is insufficient.

2) Ensuring that search committees are diverse: Having one or more racially diverse individuals on faculty search committees provides a perspective that racially homogeneous committees do not have. This perspective can make a significant difference in the likelihood that a new faculty hire will add to the diversity of the institution.

3) Factoring in a commitment to racial diversity and racial equality, as evidenced in the applicant's record of teaching and public service, as important criteria for faculty recruitment and promotion.

One additional benefit of racial diversity on faculty recruitment committees is that it provides an opportunity for faculty members from different racial groups to interact in a cooperative way toward a common goal. There may be areas of disagreement, but if these are discussed in a collaborative, mutually respectful way, there is much benefit for the participants, and for the observers. Positive interactions yield positive outcomes for everyone. The process becomes as valuable as achieving the previously identified goal.

Creating and maintaining a diverse faculty is a cornerstone for building a diverse institution. Student interactions are very important, but faculty members are the primary people that students will learn from and identify with. Without faculty diversity, there are serious limitations on institutional diversity.

Making Diversity Central to the Mission of the Institution

In order for colleges and universities to create effective diversity initiatives on their campuses, it is essential that diversity becomes central to the mission of the institution (Smith, 2015; Williams, 2013). It is also essential that individuals and groups from all levels of the institution—students, faculty, and staff—participate in the creation of the institutional diversity plan. Senior leadership is essential to this process, but all voices need to be heard. In a campus where diversity is a central value, the evidence can be found at every level, from the board of directors to the president to department chairs, faculty members, graduate and undergraduate students, admissions staff, counselors, campus police, etc.

Coordination and oversight of all these levels of commitment is a central responsibility of the Chief Diversity Officer (CDO) (Williams, 2013). This individual needs to facilitate communication and coordination of diversity activities in every arena. At the same time the CDO needs to take a leadership role in monitoring the state of institutional diversity on campus and maintaining the institution's central commitment to the value of diversity.

Diversity initiatives on college and university campuses are essential for the educational and psychological development of students, faculty, and staff. In a truly diverse climate, everyone grows.

References

Devine, P. G., Forscher, P. S., Austin, A. J., & Cox, W. T. L. (2012). Long-term reduction in implicit race bias: A prejudice habit-breaking intervention. *Journal of Experimental Social Psychology, 48*(6), 1267–1278.

Fox, H. (2001). *When race breaks out.* New York: Peter Lang.

Greenwald, A. G., McGee, D. E., & Schwartz, J. L. K. (1998). Measuring individual differences in implicit cognition: the implicit association test. *Journal of Personality and Social Psychology, 74*(6), 1464–1480.

Price, T. (2017, November 17). Affirmative action and college admissions. *CQ Researcher, 27*(41), 969–992.

Regents of the University of California vs Bakke (1978). No. 76–811, Supreme Court of the United States

Reid, F. (1995). Skin Deep. *California Newsreel,* newsreel.org/video/SKIN-DEEP

Sangillo, G. (2018). *Faculty training on inclusive pedagogy.* www.american.edu

Smith, D. G. (2015). *Diversity's promise for higher education: Making it work* (2nd Ed.). Baltimore, MD: Johns Hopkins University Press.

Teaching Tolerance. (2000). *A Place at the table.*www.tolerance.org

University of Oklahoma. (2017). www.ou.edu/web/news_2017/ou-honored-with-second-national-award-for-diversity-and-inclusion.

Wells, A. S., Fox, L., & Cordova-Cobo, D. (2016). *How racially diverse schools and classrooms can benefit all students.* New York, NY: The Century Foundation.

Williams, D. A. (2013). *Strategic diversity leadership: Activating change and transformation in higher education.* Sterling, VA: Stylus.

Chapter 6

Two Diversity Programs for Adults

Dr. Martin Luther King, Jr. believed that "like life, racial understanding is not something that we find but something that we must create...The ability of Negroes and Whites to work together, to understand each other, will not be found ready-made; it must be created by the fact of contact" (King III & King, 2001).

Dr. King's words are supported by decades of research. As we delineated in Chapter 1, the research evidence for Intergroup Contact Theory is compelling. As Martin Luther King suggested, racial understanding doesn't just happen; it must be created by positive contact over time. Our experience with multiple diversity initiatives during the past twenty years has convinced us of the wisdom of these words.

In Chapter 1 we also touched on the establishment of a Common Ingroup Identity as a vehicle through which intergroup contact reduces stereotypes and prejudice. In this chapter we expand our discussion of Common Ingroup Identity, and present two adult initiatives that illustrate how this process can help to build bridges across the racial divide.

Common Ingroup Identity

Common Ingroup Identity theory suggests that when people from different groups experience positive contact with one another, they establish a new shared identity, one that exists alongside and complements their core identity. Applied to race relations, this theory suggests that when individuals from different racial backgrounds participate together in positive experiences, they form a shared identity as members of the same, racially integrated group. They don't lose their basic group identities, but they add a new overarching identity to their understanding of the "self." Who am I? I am all these things...

Many research studies have lent support to the Common Ingroup Identity theory. In one such study (Nier, Gaertner, Dovidio, Banker, & Ward, 2001), Black interviewers approached White college students who were attending a football game and asked them to help the interviewer by completing a questionnaire. The interviewers wore hats representing one of the two teams that were playing in the game. The results showed that White students were significantly more likely to help the Black interviewer when both of them were wearing a hat of the same team. The hat seemed to lead the White students to recategorize the interviewer as part of the university in-group, leading to a greater willingness to help.

In another study (Gaertner, Mann, Murrell, & Dovidio, 1989), college students were divided into teams of three members each. The teams were given a chance to develop their own identity by working on a shared problem. Then, half of the teams were asked to join together as six member teams to work on a different problem. The teams that didn't join together continued to work on the new problem as separate three person teams. The results showed that the teams that joined together developed a sense of common group identity. When asked to evaluate members of their group, the individuals in the six member team did not show favoritism toward the members of their original three member team. In marked contrast, the members of the three member teams that continued to work separately made significantly more positive evaluations of the members of their own team than they did of the "other" team.

In a third study (Nier, et al., 2001), White college students participated in a session in which they interacted with a Black student. Half
of the White students were led to believe that they and the person they
were interacting with were separate individuals participating in the
study at the same time. The other half were told that the two participants were members of the same team. The results showed that the
White students evaluated the Black students significantly more favora-
bly when they perceived them as teammates rather than just individuals without common group connections.

These studies, and many others, lend experimental support to
Common Ingroup Identity theory. In the following sections we illustrate how this theory can help us understand the process by which
positive contact over time can lead to the reduction of stereotypes and
prejudice and increase mutual understanding and trust between individuals from different racial backgrounds.

Project Unity

The village of Oak Park, Illinois, is one of very few communities in the
United States that has made a sustained commitment to racial diversity.
Until the 1960s, the population of Oak Park was almost entirely White.
As Black families from nearby Chicago began to move in, Oak Park established a series of programs to encourage racial integration. The first
step was to discourage "White flight." Since many White homeowners were worried about their property values going down when Black
families moved in, the village bought a homeowners insurance policy.
If the value of a homeowner's property went down the insurance policy would cover the difference. To date no one has needed to file a claim
on this insurance policy. The village also established a housing office,
whose mission was to encourage anyone who inquired about moving
to Oak Park to buy or rent in ways that promote racial diversity.

The steps that Oak Park took were successful—the community has
been racially diverse for more than 50 years. Children growing up in
Oak Park attend integrated schools. Adults eat at integrated restaurants
and shop at integrated stores. Many churches have integrated congre-

gations. The process has not always been smooth, but when problems arise they are openly discussed and collectively managed.

Forming Project Unity

In their elementary school years, children in Oak Park often have integrated friendship groups. As they move into middle school and then high school, this becomes less and less the case. Two Oak Park mothers, one Black and one White, were troubled by this pattern. They attended a parent-student forum where this issue was discussed. The students participating in that discussion pointed out that their parents didn't interact much across racial lines either. Maybe that was part of the problem.

Motivated by this discussion, the two mothers broadened their inquiry to include other individuals and groups in the community in order to discern whether the problem of "resegregation" was as widespread as they imagined. They discovered that many other families shared their concern and saw this as a problem they wished could be remedied.

The two moms decided to take action. They started a new organization, Project Unity, whose mission was to bring together racially diverse Oak Park individuals and families for regular meetings at each other's homes. The meetings were a combination of social gatherings and discussions about race. The overall organization sponsored events—lectures, dances, family picnics—but most of the activity was concentrated in more intimate, ongoing small groups.

Getting Personal

Soon after moving to Oak Park, we became active in Project Unity. Our group consisted of nine individuals, four Black and five White. Initially, our monthly meetings were pleasant pot luck suppers and conversations focused on external events—primarily comparing notes on recent happenings in Oak Park and in Chicago. After a few meetings, we felt more comfortable with one another and interactions became more personal. During a conversation about the state of race relations in Oak

Park, Bob, one of the African-American members of the group, said: "I don't really trust any White people." Feeling surprised and disappointed, I (L.F.) asked Bob if that included the White members of our group. He responded: "Larry, you're Jewish. If you lived in a village where most of your neighbors were Germans, would you be able to fully trust them, really trust them, deep down inside?" I was somewhat taken aback by Bob's statement, but as I thought about it I had to admit I would probably feel the same kind of mistrust of my German neighbors that Bob felt toward his White neighbors—even those of us in the Project Unity group. Bob went on to talk about how his father would often caution him: "Don't trust Whitey, he's tricky." After hearing that repeated many times as he was growing up, along with other statements about how careful he needed to be around White people, Bob had incorporated a strong mistrust of "Whitey." That mistrust was regularly reinforced through the years by his almost daily encounters with racial stereotypes, prejudice, and discrimination.

Racial Discrimination

After the meeting in which Bob shared his mistrust of White people, the tone of the group became increasingly personal. All of us were more willing to take risks, to share our thoughts and feelings, to be vulnerable with one another. At one meeting Fred, another African-American member of the group, volunteered how upset and angry he was about an incident that had happened recently at a trade show.

Fred had just launched a new business and he was enthused about going from booth to booth with his young White employee—making connections and exploring marketing opportunities. He was frustrated, however, when the people at the first few booths looked past him and offered a warm greeting to his employee. Fred decided to set up an "experiment" by purposely approaching the subsequent booths several steps ahead of the employee. In every instance there was no acknowledgment of Fred's presence. Those managing the booths reached out around Fred to extend a welcoming hand to his White employee. There seemed to be an automatic assumption that the White man must be the business owner, the decision maker. Fred felt "invisible."

As Fred told us this story his hurt and anger were obvious in his words, tone, and facial expression. At one point he loudly exclaimed: "White people don't want Black people to succeed!" He shared a number of other examples from his life experience that had strengthened this belief.

The other members of the group responded with anger and compassion. We were furious that our talented, resilient friend had been disrespected. We shared stories of our own experiences of racial, gender, and religious bias and discrimination. The White members agreed with Fred that White people often do behave in discriminatory ways that suggest they do not want Black people to be successful. We maintained, however, that not every White person feels that way. We assured Fred that we very much wanted him to succeed and we knew from previous stories he had shared that other White friends and colleagues had been supportive of his new venture. Fred expressed appreciation for our support, and acknowledged that not all White people were the same. He maintained, however, that we were the exception.

The lengthy discussion of this incident left all of us feeling more closely connected with one another. Our common in-group identity was clearly solidifying.

Acting White

At a later meeting Denise, one of the White women in the group, talked about the verbal attacks she had been receiving after she presented the results of her PhD dissertation at the Oak Park library. Denise had interviewed students at Oak Park high school about the Black-White achievement gap at the school. As with many schools across the country Black students, on average, had lower academic achievement scores than White students. When Denise talked with Black students at the high school, many of them told her that they thought one explanation for the achievement gap was that Black students were afraid that if they studied hard and got good grades they would be accused by their peers of "acting White." When Denise presented this finding in her talk at the library she was strongly criticized by some of the Black adults in the audience, who argued that the "acting White" explanation was a way for White people to avoid facing the real cause of the achievement gap—White racism. Denise said she certainly agreed that White racism was a major cause of the problem, but insisted that what the Black students had told her should be taken seriously and that specific interventions to deal with that aspect of the problem were needed.

Our Project Unity group discussion of this issue was difficult. We all were very supportive of Denise and admiring of her determination to take seriously what the Black students had told her. We all agreed that the "acting White" phenomenon was real and needed serious attention. At the same time we understood how the Black adults in her audience would be wary of anything that could lead to a "blaming the victim" reaction. We struggled to help Denise find a way to emphasize the role of systemic racism as a major cause of the achievement gap while also insisting on the importance of helping Black students overcome the destructive consequences of the "acting White" phenomenon.

Becoming Friends

After meeting for six months, our Project Unity group began getting together between meetings to share social activities. We went to local restaurants for dinner, attended plays together, and on one occasion went to hear one of our members give a speech about labor history in Chicago. These social gatherings became an important part of our group process, deepening our personal connections to one another.

When, in 1997, the two of us moved to Southwest Michigan, we initially continued to meet with our Project Unity group every month. After a while we reduced the frequency of our participation, but still got together with the group as often as possible, either in Oak Park or by hosting them in Michigan. To this day, twenty-five years after our Project Unity group began, many of the members of that group remain among our closest friends.

Race Relations Council

As we noted earlier, in 1998 writer Alex Kotlowitz published *The Other Side of the River*, detailing the racial divide between the Southwest Michigan "twin cities" of Benton Harbor and St. Joseph. Benton Harbor is economically depressed, with a population that is more than 90% Black; St. Joseph is middle to upper class, and more than 90% White. Kotlowitz graphically described the alienation, hostility, and mistrust that characterized the relationship between these two communities.

In reaction to Kotlowitz's book, a racially diverse group of residents from both sides of the river came together to form a Race Relations Council, with a mission to build bridges across the racial divide and advocate for racial equality. Armed with our experiences in Project Unity, we became two of those founding residents.

Confronting a Crisis

Soon after the Race Relations Council was formed, the Benton Harbor-St. Joseph community faced a crisis that spoke dramatically to our concerns. The Ku Klux Klan, hoping to enlist significant support, announced their intention to hold a rally in St. Joseph. This disturbing possibility prompted spirited discussion and heated debate among the members of the Race Relations Council. What role could we play in helping the community deal with these malignant intruders?

Some Council members felt we should do nothing—ignore the event and avoid creating more publicity for the Klan. Others strongly disagreed, arguing that we should confront the Klan directly and hold a counter-rally in the immediate vicinity. A third group proposed partnering with an organization of area ministers who were planning a unity prayer service in Benton Harbor that would be held at the same time that the Klan rally was scheduled in St. Joseph.

After much discussion, the group decided to publish a lengthy letter in the local newspaper, urging area residents to take positive steps to counter the bigotry and hate-mongering of the Klan. We suggested that parents talk with their children about prejudice and intolerance, that families from both sides of the river come together to share social or recreational activities, and that individuals from all racial groups make a commitment to participate in one or more projects designed to improve the quality of life for everyone in our communities. We concluded by urging all area residents to attend the unity prayer service and demonstrate a commitment to working together to build a more diverse and inclusive community.

On the day of the event, attendance at the Klan rally was sparse. A small group of curious onlookers, a few vocal supporters, and several hecklers watched as a handful of Klan members shouted their toxic rhetoric. In dramatic contrast, less than a mile away, the church in Benton Harbor was overflowing. Large numbers of St. Joseph residents joined their Benton Harbor neighbors to create, for that day, an enthusiastic multiracial congregation. The energy in the room was infectious—this group was determined not only to send a clear message to the Klan, but also to build alliances and bridge the racial divisions between the two communities. By the end of the service, participants were energized and hopeful.

Honoring Pioneers and Unsung Heroes

Inspired by the camaraderie and commitment generated in the Unity prayer service, the Race Relations Council initiated a "Community Celebration and Awards Program," honoring individuals from the community who had made significant contributions to promoting racial equality and racial healing. We saw these "pioneers and unsung heroes" as valuable role models, and felt it was important to provide recognition and reinforcement for their work. Our plan was to hire musical entertainment, charge a small admission fee, and develop fundraising projects to promote the event. Proceeds would be used to fund two scholarships at the local community college, scholarships that would be offered to students who had demonstrated a commitment to improving race relations in their communities.

More than five hundred residents, from both sides of the river, attended the Community Celebration and Awards Program. Many who were present that day expressed strong support for regularly highlighting positive contributions and for bringing people together to celebrate diversity. In light of the program's success, the Race Relations Council decided to make it an annual event.

Forming a Multiracial Children's Choir

For the first two years of the Awards program, professional singers and musicians provided the entertainment. In planning the third celebration, one of the authors (S.F.) suggested to the organizing committee that instead of continuing that practice, we bring together children from Benton Harbor, St. Joseph, and nearby communities to form a multiracial children's choir.

With the help of two local ministers, one from Benton Harbor and one from St. Joseph, along with volunteer choir directors from both sides of the river, we organized the *All God's Children Community Choir* (see Chapter 2). Over the years All God's Children has performed on many occasions in many locations. Friendships have developed between choir members, choir parents and grandparents, and choir directors. The choir has become a musical ambassador for racial diversity and inclusion. Choir members and their families have become models for the community of what can happen when people from different racial backgrounds come together as equals to collaborate on a shared project.

Assessing Racial Attitudes and Behavior

One of the first projects that the Race Relations Council undertook was a study of race-related attitudes and behavior of residents in Benton Harbor and St. Joseph. A questionnaire was developed that asked a variety of questions about these two psychological phenomena. The questionnaires were completed by three groups of individuals from each community: (1) high school students; (2) community college students; and (3) adult church members.

The major findings from this study were:

- Meaningful conversations (ones in which each person talks about his or her thoughts and feelings) between Black and White individuals happened significantly more often between students at the community college than between high school students or adult church members.

- Socializing (sharing a meal or other social activity) between Black and White individuals happened significantly more often between students at the community college than between high school students or adult church members

- Community college students expressed more positive feelings toward people of a different race than did high school students or adult church members. They felt understood more often and were more trusting. These differences were larger for White college students than for Black college students.

The community college in Southwest Michigan is almost always the first place that Black and White people have regular contact with one another. The survey results suggest that this contact leads to greater communication and socialization, increased understanding, and increased trust, especially for White students.

Shining a Light on Home Lending Inequities

One of the major problems in the Benton Harbor community has been (and continues to be) deteriorating housing stock. Many houses are in need of significant repair; others are beyond repair, serve as a magnet for social problems, and need to be torn down.

As the Race Relations Council began to discuss housing issues, residents of Benton Harbor expressed frustration that home improvement loans, though sorely needed, were difficult to obtain. Homeowners who applied were often informed that the lending institution would not provide the loan because other properties in the neighborhood were in such poor condition. The stated rationale was that neighboring properties had to reach a certain appraised value in order to "justify the investment." Clearly, this created a vicious circle—the homeowner who wanted to improve his or her property was denied a loan because other properties in the area also needed to be improved. How then would it ever be possible to improve housing, block by block, house by house?

Benton Harbor residents also reported that loan applications for home purchases in their city were frequently denied. When they were able to purchase a home they were often unable to make needed repairs because of the difficulty obtaining a home improvement loan. As a result, property values continued to decline.

The Race Relations Council decided to explore this situation by collaborating with the Woodstock Institute, a Chicago-based group that studies lending practices in urban areas. Using Home Mortgage Disclosure Act data, which lending institutions are required to submit to the federal government, we compared the frequency of denials for home improvement and home purchase loans in Benton Harbor to those in St. Joseph. All comparisons were between applicants from the same income level—either low to moderate, middle, or upper.

The results of the study showed that the loan denial rate for individuals with the same income level was considerably higher in Benton Harbor than in St. Joseph. The difference was especially large for home improvement loan applications by low to moderate and middle income applicants. In Benton Harbor, applications for such loans from individuals with low to moderate incomes were denied 62% of the time. Middle income applicants were denied 57% of the time. Comparable denial rates in St. Joseph were 16% and 38%!

We decided to bring the study results to the attention of the local newspaper, which published them in a front-page story. Soon afterward, we convened a meeting of area lenders to discuss the findings. The lenders were defensive about their practices, but acknowledged that in order for conditions in Benton Harbor to improve, more home loans needed to be granted. They agreed to explore ways to increase the frequency of loan approvals in Benton Harbor.

In addition to working with area lenders, the Race Relations Council has partnered with other local organizations, including the local branch of Habitat for Humanity, to raise funds to improve the housing stock in Benton Harbor. This partnership succeeded in raising $25,000 to provide a one to three match for a loan from the Federal Home Loan Bank to make needed repairs and improvements to Benton Harbor houses.

Working for Equality in the Criminal Justice System

Benton Harbor and St. Joseph are located in Berrien County, where legal representation for the indigent had, until recently, been provided through contracts between the county and private attorneys. The vast majority of area attorneys avoided these contracts, primarily because of the low pay and heavy workload. Those who did accept the contracts often devoted minimal time to these cases. Since the poverty rate in Benton Harbor is much higher than in the rest of the county, African-American residents who were accused of committing crimes were much more likely to have no other choice than to use a contract attorney and, in far too many cases, receive inadequate legal representation.

In response to this problem, the Race Relations Council investigated the inequities in the criminal justice system in Berrien County and developed recommendations for change. We saw a critical need for the establishment of a Public Defender's Office, with funding equal to that of the Prosecutor's office. Members of the Council visited a number of Michigan communities that had established Public Defender offices and interviewed attorneys who had been instrumental in the creation of these offices. Based on this information, the Race Relations Council partnered with other area groups to petition the County Board to create such a resource. After much discussion and considerable delay, a Public Defender office was established for Berrien County in 2017.

The Race Relations Council also established a fruitful collaboration with a local judge, who was eager to provide a more impactful form of misdemeanor sentencing. Three White teenage boys had been brought to court for painting racial slurs on the side of a building. The judge hearing the case decided that, in addition to paying a fine, the boys would be ordered to attend a number of Race Relations Council meetings. She wanted them to experience a racially diverse group of men and women working together as allies to promote positive race relations. The boys, along with their parents, attended two meetings, and were actively involved in the process. At the conclusion of the second meeting, all of the boys expressed appreciation for the opportunity to interact with the Council, and thanked the group for helping them see things in a different light. They expressed feelings of shame, guilt, and regret about their previous behavior, and made a commitment to use their experience with the Race Relations Council as a springboard to more positive actions in the future.

Becoming Family

In the course of working together on a variety of projects, the members of the Race Relations Council have shared thoughts and feelings, hopes and fears, frustrations, anger, and delight. We have not always agreed on the best way to proceed, but disagreements have never short-circuited our commitment to the group's mission or to each other.

The intimacy of a relatively small group (15–20 individuals) has facilitated the development of personal relationships and a common group identity. In addition to our monthly meetings, sponsored forums, and fund-raising efforts, we celebrate the winter holidays and create a summer "pot-luck" barbecue. We visit each other's homes, share meals, and talk about our families, our interests, and our work. We support one another during hard times.

Over the 20 plus years since the founding of the Race Relations Council, we have become "extended family," joined together by a mutual commitment to a shared vision, and by genuine affection for one another. We recognize the limits of what a small group can accomplish, but we are convinced that the combined efforts of many such groups, working toward common goals, can lead to significant and enduring positive change.

Developing a Common In-Group Identity

Project Unity and the Race Relations Council both illustrate how people from different racial groups can come together in positive ways and develop a common in-group identity. We certainly retained our separate group identities, but we embraced an additional shared identity. Stereotypes and false beliefs were reduced as we came to know one another as individuals and, over time, as dear friends.

References

Gaertner, S. L., Mann, J., Murrell, A., & Dovidio, J. F. (1989). Reducing intergroup bias: The benefits of recategorization. *Journal of Personality and Social Psychology, 57*(2), 239–249.

King, M. L. III, & King, C. S. (2001). *The words of Martin Luther King, Jr.,* (2nd Ed.). New York, NY: William Morrow Paperbacks.

Nier, J. A., Gaertner, S. L., Dovidio, J. F., Banker, B. S., Ward, C. M. & Rust, M. C. (2001). Changing interracial evaluations and behavior: The effects of a common group identity. *Group Processes and Intergroup Relations, 4*(4), 299–316.

Chapter 7

Bridge Building Activities for Adults

There are a large number of activities that adults can pursue to build bridges across the racial divide. In this chapter we explore a variety of these activities.

Media

Movies and television shows have been a factor in the development and maintenance of racial stereotypes and prejudice (Dixon & Maddox, 2005; Johnson, Olivo, Gibson, Reed, & Ashburn-Nardo, 2009). When there are few shows or films that feature people of color, the view that they are insignificant is reinforced. When characters live in segregated worlds, segregation becomes "how things are supposed to be." When the preponderance of doctors, lawyers, executives, psychologists, etc., are White and the majority of service providers—maids, cooks, house-keepers, yard workers, etc.—are racial minorities, the belief that only White people have higher-paying jobs and that the role of racial minorities is to "serve" them is reinforced.

Fortunately, some positive shifts have occurred in recent years and we see more examples on TV and in the movies of integrated friendship groups and individual characters whose work is not determined by the color of their skin. Social psychologists have hypothesized that watching shows that contain images of positive contact between members of different racial groups has the potential to reduce racial stereotyping and prejudice (Schiappa, Gregg, & Hewes, 2005). In a study investigating this hypothesis (Cummings, 2013), a group of 183 White college students were randomly assigned to watch 15 minute segments from either: (1) a TV show in which White and Black characters are shown interacting in warm, friendly, caring ways; or (2) a TV show in which White characters only are shown interacting in similarly positive ways. Prior to watching the TV show segment, the students were asked to "sign in" with their name and contact information on a computer. During the course of this "sign in," an image of two people who were identified as students who would be the subject's "conversation partners" after they watched the TV segment flashed on the screen. These images were of same-gender African-Americans.

After the students watched the TV segment, they went to an adjoining room, ostensibly to meet with their conversation partners. When they entered the room they saw three folding chairs leaning against the wall. The experimenter asked the students to please set up one chair for him or herself and two chairs for the conversation partners. One of the main outcome variables was the distance between the White student's chair and the chairs of the two Black conversation partners.

When the chairs were set up, the students were told that their partners were delayed and that this provided an opportunity for them to fill out a group of questionnaires which asked about attitudes and feelings regarding African-Americans. When the questionnaires were completed, the researcher debriefed the students on the nature of the experiment, explaining that there were not any actual conversation partners. The experimenter thanked the students for their participation.

The results of this study demonstrated that watching the TV segment with positive interactions between Black and White characters had a significant effect on the White students' feelings and behavior. Compared to the students who watched the TV segment with positive interactions among White people only, the students who watched the segment with positive intergroup interactions demonstrated two major differences: (1) Greater willingness to be in close proximity to African-Americans and; (2) Less fear of African-Americans.

These results are encouraging. They indicate that media presentations of positive interactions between individuals from different racial groups can help to reduce anxiety about having personal contact across racial lines. As we've discussed earlier, personal contact, under the right conditions, can help to reduce racial stereotypes and prejudice.

Discussion Groups

Discussions between individuals from different racial backgrounds can be bridge builders if they are properly structured. As with all intergroup contact experiences, the core conditions of equal status and respectful cooperation are essential. Unfortunately, these conditions are not always present. A number of research studies have found that racial minorities are often marginalized in such discussions and struggle to be heard (Brown & Mistry, 2006; Shaw & Barrett-Power, 1998). When the dominant group dominates the discussion, stereotypes can be reinforced and barriers strengthened. In a constructive discussion, everyone needs to have a chance to be heard and everyone's views need to be respected, even when different people have different views. A search for greater understanding and the discovery of common ground are important elements of this process.

An example of such a discussion was reported by a group of researchers from the University of Nebraska Public Policy Center (Abdel-Monem, Bingham, Marincic, & Tomkins, 2010). One hundred volunteer participants were randomly assigned into ten discussion groups with ten individuals in each group. Sixty-eight percent of the members of each group were White, eighteen percent were Black, seven percent were Hispanic, and one to two percent were Asian, Native American, or other. All of the groups had a trained moderator, who facilitated a discussion of immigration issues. The moderator emphasized the importance of participants being genuine and fully engaged in the interaction, listening intently, speaking from their own experience, and asking questions of one another out of true curiosity and the desire to know more (Fagre & Littlejohn, 2006). Following the discussion a survey instrument was administered gauging participants' perceptions of discussion dynamics. Follow-up phone interviews were conducted with 20 of the participants. The interviewees consisted of 8 individuals randomly selected from the subsample of White participants and a total of 12 participants selected from the "co-cultural" group—5 African-Americans, 5 Hispanic-Americans, 1 Asian-American, and 1 Native American.

The questionnaire results indicated that on average both White and minority interviewees agreed or strongly agreed with each of the following statements:

Communication Quality
- As a group, we communicated respect and consideration to each member
- As a group, we gave everyone's ideas fair consideration
- I felt other members of the group listened to me
- I felt I could speak up whenever I had something to say
- As a group, we accepted differences in members' styles of interacting
- As a group, we listened to everyone's ideas
- Everyone had an equal opportunity to participate in this group
- As a group, we managed any conflicts or disagreements in a way that made it easy to continue working together

Group Effectiveness
- This group made effective use of group members' knowledge and experience
- This group was effective at generating good ideas
- This group was effective at evaluating the quality of its ideas
- This group developed positive interactions among members

Group Satisfaction
- I was satisfied with the quality of the group process
- I was satisfied with the quality of the group outcome
- I was not unhappy with the other group members
- I was satisfied with the overall quality of the group effort
- I would be willing to work with this group again

While on average both White and minority group members agreed with these questionnaire items, there were significant differences between these groups in the degree of agreement. In each of the three general categories, minority participants agreed more strongly than did the White participants.

In the interviews with the selected 20 individuals, both White and minority interviewees said they valued being exposed to diverse group members and perspectives, the respectful tone of the group interaction, the facilitator's ability to guide the interaction, and the opportunity to learn. Participants of color especially appreciated having an equal opportunity to speak in their groups and having the experience of being heard.

These results make clear the importance of discussion group moderators ensuring that each group member has an equal opportunity to speak and that interactions proceed in an egalitarian and respectful way. When this happens, all participants feel valued, heard and respected and a shared in-group identity can begin to develop.

Diversity Training

Diversity training has been defined as: "A distinct set of instructional programs aimed at facilitating positive intergroup interactions, reducing prejudice and discrimination, and enhancing the skills, knowledge, and motivation of participants to interact with diverse others" (Pendry, Driscoll, & Field, 2007). A recent meta-analytical integration (Bezrukova, Spell, Perry, & Jehn, 2016) examined the results of 260 research studies of diversity training programs, seeking to answer one major question: What are the characteristics of successful diversity training programs?

Program success was evaluated by assessing the ability of the diversity training to bring about changes in three areas:

1) "Cognitive learning—the extent to which the trainees acquire knowledge (e.g., knowledge about cultural diversity issues)"
2) "Behavioral learning—the development of trainee's skills, assessed via self-reports or implicitly identified skills (e.g., situational judgment tests) and by objective behaviors and results (e.g., performance evaluation by a manager or trained observers)"
3) "Attitudinal/Affective learning—changes in trainees' attitudes on diversity and self-efficacy (beliefs in their capacity to perform)"

The researchers also evaluated trainees' reactions to the training and to the person conducting the training. They particularly looked at whether the trainees felt that the training was effective and worthwhile.

The major results of this extensive review, along with brief comments from the two of us (in italics), are as follows:

- Overall, diversity training programs were effective at producing positive outcomes. There was, however, considerable variation among the programs (some were more effective than others). *These findings on the variation in effectiveness are an important guide for those considering adopting diversity training programs in their own setting.*
- Diversity training had the largest effect on cognitive learning, followed by behavioral learning and attitudinal/affective learning. *This finding is not surprising in that the acquisition of new information, especially if it is experienced as an intellectual exercise, is less threatening and prompts less defensiveness than attempts to examine and modify one's own attitudes and behaviors. Information doesn't necessarily prompt introspection. It is "safer" to learn about another*

group, its culture and experiences, than it is to critically evaluate our own behavioral, attitudinal, and affective responses to that group.

- Cognitive learning persisted for a long time (up to 2 years) after diversity training, but behavioral and attitudinal/affective learning tended to decay over time. *Cognitive learning is a conscious intellectual activity. Shifts in feelings and attitudes are often linked to unconscious habits, early conditioning, and affective memory. If new learning in these arenas is not reinforced over time, regression seems likely—especially in times of stress.*

- Integrated programs (part of a comprehensive diversity curriculum with multiple sessions) were more effective than stand-alone programs (one session only). This was especially true in regard to behavioral and attitudinal/affective learning. *Behavioral and affective learning require repeated reinforcement. Often layers of distortions, defenses, misunderstandings, and misinterpretations need to be shed in order to experience a different attitude and feeling about "the other." One session is not likely to be enough to bring about significant and lasting change.*

- Mandatory diversity training programs were more effective than voluntary programs at producing behavioral learning and equally effective in regard to cognitive and attitudinal/affective learning. *Those who volunteer for diversity training are likely to be those who need it the least. They have already taken the critical first step—recognizing that a problem exists! When everyone's attendance is mandatory, and the facilitators are able to overcome initial resistances, those who need diversity training the most are likely to demonstrate the greatest amount of growth, having started with the greatest amount of bias.*

- Longer diversity training programs (weeks to months to years) were more effective than shorter programs (hours). There was a strong relationship between the number of training hours and positive changes in cognitive, behavioral, and attitudinal/affective learning. *Diversity training is designed to alter long-held beliefs, attitudes, and behaviors. Because these patterns have been a part of one's identity, one's "self" for most of a lifetime, the larger the invest-*

ment of time and reparative experiences, the greater the likelihood of lasting change.

- Awareness training (focused on helping participants to be more aware of their own and other cultural assumptions, values, and biases) was less effective than Skill-building training (focused on helping participants monitor their own actions and responses to specific differences, such as identifying and overcoming interracial communication barriers). This difference was especially true for behavioral and attitudinal/affective learning. *Learning about assumptions, values, and biases is important, but paying close attention to one's own behavioral, attitudinal, and emotional reactions to events in one's life is more likely to lead to positive change. Ideally, both approaches can be used as part of a comprehensive program.*

- Trainees expressed more positive reactions to training that was voluntary rather than mandatory and that utilized a variety of different training methods (lectures, media, role play, etc). *Most adults have negative reactions to being "forced" to do something and they tend to react strongly to any situation that seems to threaten their freedom of choice or autonomous functioning. It is interesting that despite this negative reaction, mandatory diversity training still produced more positive results, on average, than voluntary training. We surmise that even though some people strongly and continuously objected to being required to participate in the training, others who initially objected became caught up in the process and were able to make important positive changes.*

Another major study (Dobbin & Kalev, 2016), based on "data from 800 U.S. firms and interviews with hundreds of line managers and executives," suggests that companies have more success promoting diversity by "easing up on control" and engaging managers in a more collaborative way. Three specific strategies are recommended: engagement, contact, and social accountability.

- **Engagement.** One approach that has been successful is inviting White managers to help with recruitment of minorities on college campuses. As the managers engage in this task, their commitment to diversity often increases. Studies have found that five years after companies institute minority recruitment policies, the proportion of Black male managers increases by 8% and the proportion of Black female managers increases by 9%.

- Another effective approach is *mentoring*. When White managers mentor minority employees, they come to know them as individuals and often become invested in their success. Mentoring programs have been shown to increase management diversity by 10% or more.

- **Contact.** As much research has demonstrated, intergroup contact under equal status conditions is an effective way to reduce stereotypes and prejudice and increase mutual understanding. One method of creating that type of contact is to bring people from different parts of a business (sales, technology, production, etc) together to work as self-managed teams to plan and complete projects. This approach is likely to increase the diversity of the working group and provide an experience of working together under equal status conditions to achieve a shared goal. As we have seen, this type of experience can lead to the development of a shared in-group identity and the reduction of stereotypes and prejudice.

  Another effective method for increasing contact between members of different groups is to rotate management trainees through departments. This kind of *cross-training* brings department heads and trainees into contact with a wider variety of people. Companies that utilize this approach increase management diversity by 3 to 7%.

- **Social Accountability.** Transparency is an effective method for promoting social accountability. When everyone knows what is happening, diversity and equality tend to increase. For example, a company found that African-American employees were consistently getting smaller raises than White employees, even though they had the same job title and performance rating. A consultant suggested posting each unit's average performance rating and pay raise by race and gender. Once this information became public, the racial difference in pay raises all but disappeared. *Discrimination thrives in darkness. Exposure to the "light of day" often moves people toward more equitable policies and behaviors.*

Corporate *diversity task forces* also promote social accountability. These task forces are assembled from multiple levels of the company. Each department has a representative on the task force. One of the responsibilities of the group is to examine, on a regular basis, diversity numbers for the company and for each department within the company and figure out what needs attention. The task force members come up with relevant solutions and take them back to their departments. The collaborative process allows departments to draw from the successes and recognize the pitfalls encountered in other departments. Knowing that a member of the department will be monitoring diversity practices has been shown to increase positive practices.

In addition to *diversity task forces*, companies can effectively promote diversity by appointing a *diversity manager*. Companies with diversity managers see, on average, increases in the number of minorities in management positions of 7% to 18% over a five year period.

Community Engagement

When communities make a commitment to build bridges across the racial divide, they have many programs to choose from. In this section, we describe two such programs.

Healing Racism Seminars

Healing Racism Seminars are educational programs designed to help participants become more aware of the history and rationale for racial prejudice and discrimination and to help them understand and change their own racial biases. Most importantly, the seminars are designed to create a safe space in which individuals can identify their own stereotypical beliefs and attitudes and recognize the ways in which their prejudices may have played out in discriminatory behaviors. The seminars are purposely small—eight to ten participants—in order to facilitate meaningful experiences and discussions. The group meets once a week for two hours over a ten week period.

The Healing Racism seminars that we participated in were led by two mixed race couples. These experienced facilitators began each meeting with a brief presentation focused upon some aspect of racism. Their talks were often followed by relevant video segments, excerpts from popular movies, or clips from TV news reports.

After these initial activities, the seminar moved to "active listening," which is at the heart of the Healing Racism experience. The group is divided into two-person subgroups and the participants take turns sharing their thoughts and feelings about the particular aspect of racism that was initially discussed by the facilitators. The listener is asked to refrain from responding in any way other than by actively and empathically listening to what the speaker is saying. Each person speaks uninterrupted for 3 minutes. In the course of doing this exercise, it quickly becomes clear how seldom we really listen to one another. Our natural tendency is to actively participate in a conversation—we are half-listening to the other person as we await our turn and prepare our response. With active listening, we are forced to really focus our attention on what the other person is saying and what he or she is feeling about the issue at hand. Initially, this is surprisingly difficult, but with a little practice it begins to feel more comfortable. The great benefit of active listening is that our ability to empathize with the thoughts and feelings being expressed by the speaker is greatly enhanced. This exercise promotes a level of emotional understanding that can be quite profound. Speakers consistently report how powerful it is to be "really listened to."

Following the active listening exercise the facilitators moderate a group discussion with all of the participants. These discussions allow everyone to share the insights they have gained through their active listening exercises and to expand on their reactions to the initial presentations. Patterns emerge in this sharing that often lead to further insights. For example, in our Healing Racism experience, Black participants consistently volunteered that it was particularly powerful for them to have the experience of being "listened to" by a White person! They reported that their usual encounters with White people typically involved being "dismissed, overlooked, interrupted, or spoken down to." The active listening exercise set up a level of equity that they had rarely encountered in their day to day lives. In response, White participants reflected upon whether they themselves might have been guilty of such actions; some reluctantly admitted that they could see themselves sometimes behaving in those dismissive ways.

At times the initial presentation is an exercise rather than a talk and/or media presentation. One such exercise is "The Walk." In this experience, everyone in the group lines up against the same wall of the meeting room. The facilitators take turns reading a series of statements that begin with: "If you have never been_____, take one step forward." The content following the "never been" phrase was a series of racially or ethnically discriminatory experiences. For example: "If you have never been denied housing because of your race or ethnicity"; "If you have never been bullied because of your race or ethnicity"; "If you have never been called a derogatory name because of your race or ethnicity," etc. After a long series of such statements, the exercise is halted, participants "freeze" in place, and everyone observes what has happened. In our Healing Racism group, the White Christian members had consistently been able to walk forward, eventually reaching the other side of the room. The White Jewish participants—the two of us—made it as far as the middle of the room. The African-American members had not been able to move at all! The emotional impact of that visual image was powerful, and painful. We all knew intellectually about the ubiquity of racism, but this exercise really brought it home. The discussion that followed was emotionally charged and fruitful for all concerned. One exchange, between a White and Black member of the group, has stayed with us for a long time:

> "I knew discrimination existed, but I don't think I ever FELT it before!"
> "Well now you see what it looks like...here *we* are...still against the damn wall!"

Over the ten weeks of the Healing Racism Seminars stereotypes faded, connections solidified, and our group became very close. Racial distance gave way to shared emotional experiences. Racial stereotypes gave way to deeper understanding of each other as individuals. During our time together we developed a shared group identity—the Healing Racism group. Many of the relationships formed in that group experience have continued over time.

Council for World Class Communities

A few years after the Race Relations Council was formed, a much larger initiative was begun by the CEO of Whirlpool Corporation, whose international headquarters is located in Benton Harbor. Whirlpool had made a commitment to create and sustain a diverse corps of employees at every level of their operation. They were encountering difficulties recruiting talent from other parts of the United States and beyond. It became clear that something needed to be done to change the climate within their organization and in the highly segregated communities that surround it. With this in mind, Whirlpool hired a diversity consulting firm to coordinate their initiative, which they called the *Council for World Class Communities* (CWCC).

The CWCC utilized a variety of formats in an effort to reduce the racial segregation, alienation, and hostility in Southwest Michigan and to increase the level of mutual respect, understanding, and sense of common purpose. These formats included speakers, media presentations, group discussions, and planning retreats. Each format was designed to complement and reinforce the others.

A powerful example drawn from the speakers format involved two football coaches, Herman Boone and Bill Yoast, whose story had been told in the award-winning film *Remember the Titans*. This film depicted the impact of a court-ordered unification of a Black and a White high school in Virginia. At a local CWCC event, both coaches talked about the challenges they faced in trying to bring together Black and White athletes to form a winning football team. They described the resistance they encountered from some of the players and from assorted adults in the community. They detailed their efforts to help initially resistant Black and White football players gradually learn to work together as equals toward a shared goal—winning football games. They talked about how, over time, the hostility of most (though not all) community members was reduced through their shared interest in seeing the hometown team do well in the state tournament.

After their presentation, the coaches answered questions from the audience. Many of the questions came from high school students, who saw themselves in the characters of the film. The questions stimulated further discussion about the ways in which the integration process proceeded. The coaches emphasized the importance of equal status and staying focused on the shared goal. Those elements were, in their minds, critical for their significant success.

In addition to speakers and discussions, the CWCC organized more than two hundred people into a variety of work groups or "domains." Community members were encouraged to participate in the domain that they most closely identified with. Education, Health, Faith, Business, Government, and Community Outreach were among the domains. Each group was made up of a diverse cross section of individuals living in Southwest Michigan. Their assignment was to identify concerns or problem areas and generate ideas for possible solutions. There were regular "report outs" so that all participants were informed about the process and "product" of each domain.

The two of us joined the Community Outreach Domain and one of us (S.F.) co-chaired this group, along with an African-American teacher. Our group discussions were spirited and purposefully inclusive— everyone was given an equal opportunity to share their thoughts and feelings. Domain members didn't always agree but we dealt with one another in respectful ways. Though we came from a wide variety of racial, ethnic, religious, and socioeconomic backgrounds, we were able to coalesce around common concerns and generate potential solutions.

Over time, the CWCC project succeeded in establishing meaningful connections between individuals from different racial groups.

People got to know one another as they worked together to accomplish shared goals. Not all goals were achieved, but the process was productive. Friendships and alliances were established that became vital to other projects that followed. For example, relationships between pastors and church activists that formed in the Faith Domain often led to ongoing alliances between churches on both sides of the river. Shared services, picnics, and projects in some instances continue years after the CWCC initiative ended. Another example: Relationships formed in the Community Outreach Domain, as well as the larger CWCC contexts, proved to be very helpful to the Calling All Colors program. Cornerstone Alliance, the local Economic Development organization, agreed to provide office space for the Calling All Colors Program Director and offered much-needed bookkeeping services for the program. In addition, many CWCC participants became active supporters of Calling All Colors, providing yearly contributions and attending special events.

The community benefitted from the presence of newly-formed human connections. The overall climate improved as separation and alienation diminished.

Role of Contact Theory

The activities and initiatives that we have described in this chapter—and in the previous two chapters—succeeded, in large measure, because they adhered to the principles of Intergroup Contact Theory. They were careful to foster personal interactions, to ensure equal status for all participants, to develop shared goals, to pursue those goals in ways that fostered cooperation, and to secure validation from and collaboration with relevant authorities. In the next chapter we examine in greater detail the ways in which these principles guided the formation and development of these projects.

References

Abdel-Monem, T., Bingham, S., Marincic, J., & Tomkins, A. (2010). Deliberation and diversity: Perceptions of small group discussions by race and ethnicity. *Small Group Research, 41*(6), 746–776.

Bezrukova, K., Spell, C. S., Perry, J. L., & Jehn, K. A. (2016). A meta-analytical integration of over 40 years of research on diversity training evaluation. *Psychological Bulletin, 142*(11), 1227–1274.

Brown, A., & Mistry, T. (2006). Group work with "mixed membership" groups: Issues of race and gender. *Social Work with Groups, 28*(3–4), 133–148.

Cummings, H.M. (2013). (Dissertation) Improving intergroup relations through parasocial contact: An examination of how pro-social television can heal race relations between black and white Americans. Dept. of Communication Studies, University of Michigan, Ann Arbor, Michigan, deepblue.lib.umich.edu, *maylene_1.pdf*

Dixon, T. L., & Maddox, K. B. (2005). Skin tone, crime news, and social reality judgments: Priming the stereotype of the dark and dangerous black criminal. *Journal of Applied Social Psychology, 35*(8), 1555–1570.

Dobbin, F., & Kalev, A. (2016). Why diversity programs fail. *Harvard Business Review, 94*(7), 52–60.

Fagre, L., & Littlejohn, J. (2006). Difficult dialogues at the university of Nebraska at Omaha: Resource guide (Unpublished Manuscript), Public Dialogue Consortium

Johnson, J. D., Olivo, N., Gibson, N., Reed, W., & Ashburn-Nardo, L. (2009). Priming media stereotypes reduces support for social welfare policies: the mediating role of empathy. *Personality and Social Psychology Bulletin, 35*(4), 463–476.

Pendry, L. F., Driscoll, D. M., & Field, S. (2007). Diversity training: Putting theory into practice. *Journal of Occupational and Organizational Psychology, 80,* 27–50.

Schiappa, E., Gregg, P. B., & Hewes, D. E. (2005). The parasocial contact hypothesis. *Communication Monographs, 72*(1), 92–115.

Shaw, J. B., & Barrett-Power, E. (1998). The effects of diversity on small work group processes and performance. *Human Relations, 51*(10), 1307–1325.

Chapter 8

Intergroup Contact Conditions in College Student and Adult Initiatives

Intergroup Contact Theory provides the foundation for the programs and activities we have described in the previous three chapters. In this chapter we explore in greater depth the ways in which Contact Theory conditions are exemplified in these bridge building initiatives.

Personal Acquaintance

College Courses

Diversity-related college courses can promote personal interactions among students in a variety of ways, including: small class size (20 or less); frequent opportunities for discussions—both whole class discussions and smaller discussion groups of two to four students; facilitation of discussions by faculty trained in diversity education; and sharing of written assignments, especially those that involve students' thoughts, feelings, and interactions with others from backgrounds different from their own. In addition, providing experiences like "The Walk," which we described in our earlier discussion of Healing Racism, can allow students to share an "aha" moment as they physically position themselves in ways that reflect society's discriminatory practices.

In our course, The Psychology of Stereotypes and Prejudice, some of the most important moments in the development of personal connections have occurred when students have shared their experiences interviewing someone from a different racial background. Since this assignment occurs at a time when the course is well underway, students have mastered some of the concepts, recognize the class as a "safe space," and have a greater willingness to take risks. Their sharing, therefore, involves more revelations about their own biases and how they experienced them during and after the interview. Fellow students often offer supportive feedback regarding the student's willingness to "tell us something about yourself that you don't feel good about." Students from the same background as the person being interviewed often express appreciation for the empathic portrayal of the interviewee. Discussions around the interview lead to strengthening of the interpersonal connections between our students.

Project Unity

Project Unity was formed for the purpose of promoting personal acquaintance among individuals from different racial groups. Meeting at members' homes introduces an element of familiarity, as does the personal sharing that takes place following the initial, more tentative, period of "breaking the ice." Talking openly about life experiences, personal feelings and thoughts promotes connection, even when that sharing leads to difficult, emotionally-charged discussions. The willingness to "hang in there," to talk it through and find common ground, leads to improved understanding of each perspective and greater closeness between members of the group. Personal connection is reinforced and expanded during the group's shared social activities, when individuals can "let their hair down" and interact in a more informal way. At Project Unity's anniversary celebration, members of our "home group" gravitated toward interaction with each other, sharing a table for the meal and even taking some turns on the dance floor. It was clear that the "personal acquaintance" condition had been achieved.

Race Relations Council

The *Race Relations Council* is a project-oriented group, but the process of sharing ideas about specific problems and possible solutions has produced a great deal of personal interaction. For example, in a recent meeting the group was discussing the cumulative negative effects of slavery and Jim Crow segregation on the psychological, physical, and economic health of African-Americans. Everyone agreed that this was a serious problem that required serious solutions, and we brainstormed about how the Race Relations Council might contribute to this effort. We also agreed, however, that some Black individuals and families have managed to succeed despite the headwinds created by racial discrimination. Two members of the group, African-American sisters who were both retired educators, talked about their experiences growing up in a family in which the parents "never talked or acted like White people were in any way superior to us." They shared that their commitment to educational success often prompted bullying from some of their peers, who accused them of "acting White." The strength and determination displayed by these women were inspiring to everyone in the group. The level of sharing and admiring responses reflected the closeness we have achieved with one another.

Healing Racism Seminars

Healing Racism Seminars facilitate personal connections by keeping the group small (less than 20 people), dividing into two-person subgroups for "active listening" experiences; sharing powerful activities like "The Walk"; and discussing personal reactions to video and film presentations, active listening experiences, and group activities. The frequency of the weekly group meetings and the 12-week length of the seminar both contribute to facilitating personal interactions. By the time the process is finished, the members of the group have formed deep personal connections. Those connections often last far beyond the structure of the program. Many group members participate in a "Cousins Club" (reflecting the idea that we are all related if we look back far enough) made up of alumni from various Healing Racism seminars.

Equal Status

College Courses

College courses on diversity are based on the principle of equal status. Instructors of such courses need to ensure that every student has an equal opportunity to participate in class discussions, that such discussions are closely monitored to prevent anyone from being bullied or "shouted down," and that the instructor does not exhibit any bias in his or her management of the class. Not every student will participate in the same way. Some will want to talk a lot, some very little. Some will be very emotional, some will express little emotion. All of these variations need to be respected. Students need to feel that their way of participating is equal to the ways of other members of the class. Most importantly, instructors need to carefully monitor their own implicit biases and make sure that these are not expressed in their interactions with their students. As students become more knowledgeable about the issues at hand, they too can monitor classroom interactions and point out any inequities that may appear. The classroom becomes a safe arena in which students can develop their skill at spotting inequality in other contexts.

Project Unity

Project Unity promotes equal status by including approximately equal numbers of White and Non-White participants, alternating meetings between participants' homes, sharing group facilitation by asking whoever is hosting the meeting to be the facilitator, and focusing discussions on group members' feelings and thoughts about racial inequality and racial healing. When considering leadership roles in the larger organization, members exhibit consciousness about how these roles are distributed. For example, the organization was started by two women, one Black and one White. Efforts are made to continue this form of leadership—an equal partnership between Black and White participants.

Race Relations Council

The *Race Relations Council* maintains equal status by electing Chairpersons from different racial groups, discussing ways to reduce racial inequality, and by presenting programs with mixed-race panels. There is, within the group, a conscious effort to underscore the value of our collaboration and to identify the value added by each member's contribution. The perspective gained by hearing and acknowledging our race-related differences in life experience has been enormously enriching.

Healing Racism Seminars

In *Healing Racism Seminars* the condition of equal status is established at the outset when facilitators from different racial groups present the fundamental assertion that *all* of us harbor stereotypes and prejudice, that *all* of us have been influenced by our environment, and that we *all* operate with some explicit and implicit biases. The assumption that "everyone has work to do" sets the stage as participants view the same videos, hear the same presentations, and participate in the same type of "active listening" partnerships. Facilitators ensure that group discussions provide equal opportunities for participation from all members. Since much of the content of the seminars focuses on inequality in our society, the discussions understandably address equal status concerns as they appear in both the content and in the process of the group.

Shared Goals and Cooperative Interaction

College Courses

Students who enroll in *diversity-related college courses* generally do so because they are interested in learning about diversity. Some, but not all, are also interested in learning about their own explicit and implicit racial biases.

In our course, we begin by having students introduce themselves and ask them to say a few words about what their goals are for the course. Most students talk about gaining information about the topic;

some identify increased knowledge of their own biases as a goal. In this first meeting we sometimes encounter a student who asserts that: "I'm here because I'm concerned about the problem...but it's not *my* problem."

Following introductions we typically share the video "A Place at the Table," which we discussed in Chapter 5, and then ask students to talk about the thoughts and feelings that emerged as they watched the video. During the course of our discussion, the class begins to recognize that sharing personal reactions is going to be an important part of this course. Some students resist this aspect of our process, but most become invested in it. After several meetings there is general consensus that we share the goals of increasing our knowledge about the subject and about ourselves.

Initially, students' offerings of internal reactions are tentative and superficial, often couched in generalizations. For example, "I reacted like most people do...with some sadness and anger about the past." Over time, however, there is greater sharing of more personal reactions, including more specific information about students' own racial biases. During discussions, students are generally very supportive of one another, but on occasion disagreements emerge. During those moments, we carefully monitor the discussion—and intervene if necessary—to make sure that everyone gets a chance to speak their mind and that everyone is treated with respect. Interestingly, these discussions, which can get emotionally charged, often end up strengthening the level of closeness and cooperation in the group. Students don't always reach easy or complete agreement, but they do end up with a greater understanding of one another's point of view, and greater commitment to honest sharing of their thoughts and feelings.

Project Unity

The goals of *Project Unity* are clearly defined—bringing together people from different racial backgrounds to help bridge the racial divide. In pursuit of those goals, each Project Unity group agrees to collaborate by meeting in each other's homes to discuss race-related issues, in Oak Park and in the broader society. An implied goal is to share thoughts, feelings, and life experiences in ways that deepen connections and foster friendships. As with college student discussions, this process usually proceeds in a relatively comfortable, collaborative way but conversations can sometimes become difficult. Emotions can run high, and disagreements can arise. During these moments the group needs to address the discord, pause to remember the shared goals, and collaborate on ways to get back on track with more constructive dialogue. This process can result in closer bonds within the group and expanded communication skills to employ in the larger community.

Another form of collaboration in Project Unity is evident in the planning and sharing of social events. Group members offer ideas about what events might be good to pursue and the group reaches consensus. Over time, different members offer a wide variety of ideas—dinner at an ethnic restaurant, seeing a play about racial issues, sharing a concert, attending a group member's talk, etc. The process of working together on social events contributes to a feeling of group identity.

One of our fondest memories of Project Unity came after our move to Southwest Michigan. It was our "turn" to host and the group caravanned to our new home—potluck dishes, swimsuits, and musical instruments in hand. All members contributed to the success of the day, a day that culminated in an enthusiastic songfest on the beach. Listeners and onlookers commented upon our atypical "family" of performers. In that moment, we did indeed feel like a family—our shared goal was clearly coming to fruition.

Race Relations Council

The Race Relations Council has two major goals: racial healing and racial justice. Individuals join the group because they are committed to these clearly identified goals. The process of working together to find solutions in these two major problem areas requires a great deal of collaboration. Whether the issue is effectively countering a rally of the Ku Klux Klan, honoring pioneers and unsung heroes, starting a multiracial children's choir, surveying the community about racial attitudes and behaviors, consulting with the local hospital to reduce implicit racial bias, or lobbying for a fully-funded Public Defender's office, Race Relations Council members work together to analyze the problem, come up with proposed solutions, and turn those plans into action. Each member of the group contributes his or her ideas and special talents to this process. All members collaborate on implementation. Although different people take responsibility for different tasks, everyone contributes to the overall effort.

The process of collaborating on racial justice issues is an important vehicle for promoting racial healing. Black council members have described what they experience as a prevalent feeling in African-American communities: "White people just don't give a damn about racial injustice." White council members describe a stereotype they have encountered: "Black people are just angry—they don't want to do the work to make things better." As Black and White Race Relations Council members work together to discuss and then implement proposed solutions for identified problems, these types of racial stereotypes and prejudice are diminished and mutual understanding and respect increase.

Healing Racism

Healing Racism is designed to help participants gain a greater understanding of prejudice and discrimination and of their own implicit and explicit racial biases. Since the goals are clearly stated in the program's outreach efforts, those who "sign on" have already committed to many of those shared goals. They may not, however, be totally committed to a deep exploration of their own biases. It usually takes some time for that goal to be fully embraced.

Collaboration among the participants is an essential element of this experience. Individuals need to work together to practice "active listening" and to participate in constructive discussions of their reactions to this exercise and to the verbal and media presentations that make up the beginning of each seminar. They also need to collaborate on the activities, like "The Walk," that provide vivid illustrations of the phenomena brought to light in the Healing Racism seminars. Cooperative interaction and collaboration are at the center of the racial healing process.

Support from Relevant Authorities

College Courses

In order to effectively teach a *college diversity course*, support from the administration and department heads is essential. The addition of diversity-related courses can stimulate controversy. Academic institutions can be reluctant to introduce content that might be "disturbing" to some in the community that they serve. There may be resistance from students or their families, from faculty, staff, or alumni. A commitment from the department head, the academic dean, and the president of the college is important in securing a spot in the curriculum and maintaining that presence, even in the face of opposition. The message from all of these authorities needs to be that the college is committed to diversity education, is supportive of this particular effort, and recognizes the alignment of diversity with other fundamental values of the institution.

Once the course is underway, administrative support needs to continue. Academic advisers need to be familiar with the content and process of the course so they can answer students' questions. The department head also needs to be familiar with the course material in case questions arise about why or how a particular issue is being addressed (for example, the issue of White privilege can at times arouse strong emotional resistance). Coordination and communication between the instructor(s) and the administration needs to be clear and consistent. Everyone needs to be on the same page about the importance of diversity education. Without that consensus it is difficult for such courses to endure.

Project Unity

Project Unity was started by two women in the Oak Park community who wanted to promote increased personal contact between Black and White residents. This was a private initiative, but it was built on the public commitment to racial integration that the community of Oak Park had made many years before. Oak Park was, and still is, one of very few racially integrated communities in the United States. Racial integration, however, is more than just people from different racial backgrounds living in the same community. The founders of Project Unity recognized that people from different racial groups who lived in Oak Park were not having much personal contact with one another. They were determined to start an organization whose mission was to bring people together in social settings and give them an opportunity to really get to know one another. To publicize their new organization they contacted the two local community newspapers, the Oak Leaves and the Wednesday Journal, both of which ran articles about Project Unity. The widely read papers gave an air of credibility to the newly launched initiative. The papers, along with flyers posted in "high traffic areas," became the primary method by which Project Unity attracted members. People read about the program and used the contact number to ask questions and obtain additional information. Without the support of the Oak Leaves and Wednesday Journal, Project Unity would have had a much more difficult time getting launched. Oak Park residents responded to the newspaper articles because they trusted their papers to share information about important events happening in their community. Over the years, these papers continued to support Project Unity by publishing articles about regular events that the organization was sponsoring—lectures, movies, anniversary dinners, etc. The partnership that Project Unity forged with the Oak Leaves and Wednesday Journal has been an essential support during the entire life of the organization.

Race Relations Council

The Race Relations Council was founded by a group of private citizens, but was assisted by two public institutions—Lake Michigan College (LMC) and Cornerstone Alliance, the major economic development organization in Southwest Michigan. The initial meeting of the group was held at the college, and the initial Board Chair was LMC's Senior Vice President. After the first meeting, the group shifted locations to the Cornerstone Alliance building, at the invitation of that organization's director, who was a founding member of the Council. We continued to meet at Cornerstone for many years.

As the Race Relations Council planned and executed different projects, other well-established organizations also provided assistance. When we finished designing our survey of racial attitudes and behavior, we reached out to one of the local high schools, to Lake Michigan College, and to an area church. All of these institutions were very helpful during the data collection process. Cornerstone Alliance was again on board during the data analysis phase of the project. When the study was complete, our local newspaper, the Herald-Palladium, published the results on their front page.

When the Council conducted our "home loan" study we were greatly assisted by the Woodstock Group, which is based in Chicago. After the results of this study were compiled, the Herald-Palladium again published a compelling front page article about the study. This was particularly significant because the findings exposed racial disparities in lending practices by local financial institutions.

The Race Relations Council has periodically received support from local ministers, school principals, and the local hospital. After the Racial Attitudes and Behavior study was published in the local paper, the University of Michigan reached out to the council and requested a copy of the raw data for their Michigan Archives Library so that scholars could have access to the data for subsequent analyses. All of these individuals and institutions have helped to validate and reinforce the work of the Race Relations Council. Each "endorsement" enhanced the credibility of the organization and opened doors for future endeavors.

Healing Racism Seminars

Healing Racism Seminars grew out of the work of the Institutes for the Healing of Racism and the writings of Nathan Rutstein and Reginald Newkirk (Newkirk & Rutstein, 2000; Rutstein, 1988). These pioneers established the principles and basic format for the seminars and then helped others learn to be seminar facilitators. The Healing Racism seminars in Southwest Michigan are part of a network of similar initiatives, in Michigan and around the country. Periodically, there are regional and national conferences in which individuals who have participated in the Healing Racism program gather to hear speakers, watch videos, and share discussions about their experiences. These gatherings help to extend and reinforce the Healing Racism experience. Links to the national organization add credibility to local initiatives.

The work of our local Healing Racism seminars group has been supported by a number of area churches, by our local hospital, and by the Baha'i faith community in our region. A central tenet of the Baha'i faith is the oneness of humanity and a central mission of its followers is the elimination of racism. It is not surprising then that in our area the Baha'i community has been very affirming of the work of the Healing Racism Seminars. The contributions of the faith community and the volunteering of meeting space by the hospital enhanced the perception of these seminars as valuable resources.

Repeated Contact Over Time

In order for intergroup contact to be most effective in reducing stereotypes, prejudice, and discrimination, the contact needs to be repeated over time. In *diversity courses*, students and faculty are in contact with each other one or more times a week for one or more semesters. *Project Unity* participants get together on a monthly basis for an extended period of time—some groups continue for years. *Race Relations Council* members meet once a month for multiple years. Participants in *Healing Racism* have weekly meetings for twelve weeks, and some have periodic follow up gatherings ("Cousins Club") for much longer. These extended contacts greatly increase the likelihood that intergroup friendships will develop and stereotypes and prejudice will be reduced. Enduring friendships, as we have previously noted, are the most powerful means for reducing racial bias.

Establishing a Common Ingroup Identity

College Courses

Students in *college diversity courses* start out as a group of individuals with a variety of different racial and ethnic identities. Over time, when the course goes well, they come to experience an overarching shared identity as people who are committed to understanding and reducing racial stereotypes and prejudices, including the ones they have become aware of in themselves. Instructors can facilitate this process in a number of ways. In our course, we have found it helpful to keep the size of the class small—no more than twenty students. The small class size encourages more personal contact and more meaningful discussions. Instructors positively reinforce sharing of experiences and insights and point out common threads in the fabric of students' stories.

We have also found it helpful to ask students to interview someone from a racial group different from their own and to pay close attention to their thoughts and feelings about the interview and the person they are interviewing. Sharing those reactions with the class, especially when they include increased awareness of one's own stereotypes and prejudice, has proven to be a very powerful means for helping to create a shared group identity. Classmates often volunteer their own identification with either the interviewer or the individual being interviewed. The "risk taking" by all parties strengthens the connections between classmates and the feeling that "we're all in this together." The awareness that "most of the community doesn't talk about the elephant in the living room" contributes to the shared group identity.

Another contribution comes from resolving disagreements in a positive way. When disagreements arise, as they inevitably do, our efforts are directed toward helping the students learn how to actively listen to what the other person is saying, empathically reflect on what that person is feeling, actively search for any points of agreement, and express their thoughts and feelings in a respectful way—even when feelings are strong. Ideally, at the end of such discussions, everyone in the class has a clearer understanding of each person's perspective on the issue at hand, as well as the varied emotional reactions to that issue. The ability to tolerate differences and embrace similarities is an important skill necessary for fully engaging with others.

Project Unity

Project Unity participants start out with a shared desire to bridge the racial divide, but with distinct racial and ethnic identities. Sometimes those separate identities can lead to difficult discussions. For example, I (L.F.) entered my first Project Unity meeting determined to confront African-American participants with the anti-semitism of Minister Louis Farrakhan. I imagined myself asking such questions as: "How can you respect someone who talks that way about Jews?" I did bring the subject up in the first meeting and I was struck with how complicated the issue was for Black members of the group. On one hand, they condemned Farrakhan's anti-semitic remarks. On the other hand, they greatly valued his commitment to improving the lives of African-Americans by helping young people increase their self-esteem and achieve success, first in school and later in the world of work. As we discussed this issue, we all began to understand one another at a deeper and more meaningful level. African-American group members could identify with being on the receiving end of demeaning and hostile remarks. As a Jew, I could identify with the critical need for "minority" leaders to encourage youth to rise above the stereotypes and prejudices and be all that they could be. Those identifications formed the basis for our shared empathic connections.

During the course of monthly meetings, interspersed with social experiences, we began to acquire a shared group identity. We came to see ourselves as members of "Project Unity," a group strongly committed to removing racial barriers and making a positive difference in the community.

Race Relations Council

The *Race Relations Council* came together in response to the publication of Alex Koltlowitz's book *The Other Side of the River*, which graphically highlighted the racial disparities, hostility, and mistrust that characterized the "Twin Cities" of Benton Harbor and St. Joseph. In the initial meeting of that group, some of the tensions between these communities were quite apparent. Midway through the meeting, after many Benton Harbor residents had detailed a variety of ways in which racial discrimination affected their daily lives, a White man from St. Joseph raised his hand and said "I think we should stop dwelling on the past. Things are *so* much better than they used to be." In response, a Black woman from Benton Harbor replied: "This makes me *so* mad. White people are always telling us to: 'Get over it, things are not as bad as they used to be,' or 'I'm not responsible for the problem—I didn't own any slaves.'" One of the authors (S. F.) commented: "I don't think White people ought to be telling Black people that things are not as bad as they used to be. We need to acknowledge the impact of what happened in the past and we need to recognize the bad things that are happening right now. Maybe then we can take positive action to make things better."

More than fifty people attended that first Race Relations Council meeting. At the second meeting, there were only twenty. When attendees had been asked to commit to participate in ongoing meetings focused on specific problem areas, many expressed ambivalence—"I'm too busy to take on anything else"; "What good will it do?"; "We've been here before." It seemed to be much easier to attend an initial venting and brainstorming meeting than to make a commitment to an ongoing problem-solving initiative.

Those who remained, though, comprised a racially diverse group who were strongly committed to working together to develop ideas and actions for improving the state of race relations in southwest Michigan. Over more than twenty years, the members of the Council have formed very close relationships. We have worked together on numerous projects, we have celebrated holidays and shared potluck suppers, we have attended concerts, lectures, and forums together, and we have developed a shared identity. These bonds were strengthened during crises like the KKK rally in St. Joseph and an outbreak of violence following the death of a Benton Harbor resident fleeing the police. The Council's sharing of thoughts and feelings about these incidents and our collaborating on appropriate group responses revealed the level of intimacy and trust that had developed over time.

Healing Racism

The *Healing Racism* experience is very compelling. The frequency of the meetings and the evocative nature of the presentations, videos, and exercises draw the group together. Healing Racism is not an intellectual exercise. Though there is certainly learning involved, much of the experience is emotionally charged and participants are asked to be "fully present" throughout the sessions. Individuals soon begin to look forward to seeing other members of the group at upcoming meetings. Some have commented that the intensity of the material and the interpersonal exchanges can make relationships outside the group "feel superficial."

The "active listening" exercises are particularly important in promoting group cohesiveness. The experience of listening without responding is eye-opening. Talking about your feelings and thoughts to someone who is intently listening is gratifying. Participating in exercises like "The Walk" fosters empathy and draws members closer together. Group discussions provide an opportunity for everyone to express themselves and to be heard and for individuals to develop greater understanding of differing experiences. The "Cousins Club" gatherings which follow the seminars feel like family reunions, a gathering of the Healing Racism clan. The strength of the shared group identity is very clear on those occasions.

Indirect Contact

In *college diversity classes*, students not only interact directly with other students and faculty from different racial backgrounds, they also have indirect contact through their observations of other individuals participating in such interactions. Some of this indirect contact comes from watching films or videos in which students from different racial groups interact with one another. Indirect contact also comes from observing their classmates interacting with each other and with the instructors across racial lines. These observations can affect students in two ways: (1) Observing intergroup contact can reduce anxiety about participating in that kind of contact oneself; and (2) Observing such contact can, in and of itself, have a prejudice-reducing effect.

Indirect contact occurs in *Project Unity* when participants observe intergroup interactions between other members of the group. We were aware in our Project Unity experience that some members forged connections across racial lines more quickly than others. In later discussions, the more hesitant participants indicated that their observations of the developing ease in those early interactions led to a greater willingness on their part to "run the risk": "If Fred could open up like that to Pat, maybe I could talk a little more about what's going on with me."

When Project Unity members participate in outside social activities, they provide opportunities for people at restaurants, plays, lectures, etc., to benefit from indirect contact as they observe interactions between group members from different racial backgrounds. Another form of indirect contact occurs when articles and photos of Project Unity groups appear in the local papers or television news stories. Viewers can be affected by these visual images even if they are not consciously aware of what they are taking in. Each of these circumstances allows Project Unity to model positive interaction across racial lines.

The *Race Relations Council* provides a similar model when members share a meal at a local restaurant, sponsor community awards celebrations, participate in forums about race relations, or attend a performance by the All God's Children choir. The friendships among the group members are very evident in these situations. We are often told that observing the interactions between Race Relations Council members has inspired others to seek out opportunities to get to know individuals from different racial backgrounds. In some cases, observers have been inspired enough to join the Council themselves.

Healing Racism Seminars also periodically provide opportunities for nonparticipants to experience intergroup contact indirectly. When our Healing Racism group gathered for weekly seminars at Lakeland Hospital, our greetings were warm and open. People working at the hospital or visiting friends or relatives were clearly surprised to see such warmth between people from different racial groups—a phenomenon rarely experienced in our highly segregated community. When we attended conferences, something similar took place. As people watched our interactions, many seemed moved by the intergroup contact they were observing.

In all of these initiatives, a common group identity has developed. Each participant has expanded and enriched his or her individual identity to include a shared identity as a member of a multiracial group committed to bridging the racial divide.

References

Newkirk, R., & Rutstein, N. (2000). *Racial healing: The institutes for the healing of racism.* Albion, MI: National Resource Center for the Healing of Racism.

Rutstein, N. (1988). *To be one: A battle against racism.* Bahais: George Ronald.

Chapter 9

What Gets in the Way?

Building bridges across the racial divide requires commitment, determination, patience, and resiliency. As with building physical bridges, there are multiple obstacles that must be overcome in order to change the landscape. In this chapter we identify those obstacles and present strategies for overcoming them and facilitating positive social change.

A variety of different obstacles stand in the way of people becoming engaged in racial diversity initiatives. These obstacles can be divided into two major categories: perceptual obstacles and emotional obstacles.

Perceptual Obstacles

Some obstacles are a result of differences in how individuals perceive the world and themselves. These perceptual differences may be conscious or unconscious. Differences in perception can be powerful barriers to bridge building initiatives. It is critical that individuals leading these efforts become knowledgeable about and sensitive to perceptual differences between groups of participants. The language used and the structure of the process must reflect this sensitivity in order for any project to be successful.

Different Perceptions of Racial Discrimination

White and non-White Americans have dramatically different perceptions of the frequency and severity of racial discrimination. A February, 2017 poll by the Public Religion Research Institute found that 87% of Black Americans believe that Black people face "a lot" of discrimination in the United States, while a majority of White people (51%) disagree (Struyk, 2017). In a March, 2017 Quinnipiac University poll, 66% of non-Whites (Blacks, Latinos/Latinas, Asian-Americans, Native Americans and Pacific Islanders) labeled racial prejudice a "very serious problem," while only 39% of Whites felt the same way (Struyk, 2017). These differences in perception influence how White and non-White people feel about race relations initiatives. If your perception is that racial prejudice and discrimination are not serious problems, you are likely to be resistant to investing time and energy in efforts to reduce these "non-problems." You may also resent racial minorities for insisting that prejudice and discrimination are widespread in many sectors of American society.

Many White people don't see the racial divide as a problem in their lives and they don't feel any obligation to do anything about it. Some still see racial segregation as "just the way things are supposed to be." For example, soon after moving to Southwest Michigan, we encountered a White man from St. Joseph who commented: "There is no race problem in this area. Benton Harbor people just need to stay in Benton Harbor and St. Joe people need to stay in St. Joe." Sadly, we discovered that many other White people in our area echoed this man's sentiments.

Other White people *minimize* the problem, arguing: "Why are you people always harping on the past, things are better now"; "There's a Black girl in my daughter's class at school, and a Black boy on my son's rocket football team"; "You ought a just let it go!"

The refusal of many White people to recognize and grapple with the racial divide may be rooted in the desire, conscious or unconscious, to preserve their "favored status" of White privilege and/or in anxiety about social changes (Craig & Richeson, 2014; Knowles, Lowery, Chow, & Unzueta, 2014; Sidanius, Cotterill, Sheehy-Skeffington, Kteily, & Carvacho, 2016).

Individuals from racial minority groups are often resentful of White people's denial of racial barriers. Many see this denial as a deliberate effort to maintain racial inequality. Resentment reduces their motivation to interact with White people, who are often viewed as "the oppressors." While other people of color may not see such malevolent motives, they argue that denial and minimization are a result of White people "not caring about the lives we lead." All of these reactions can become obstacles to building bridges across the racial divide.

Denial of Racial Stereotypes and Prejudice

Along with minimizing the degree of racial separation, racial discrimination, and White privilege that exist in our society, many White people minimize their own racial biases. "I don't have a racist bone in my body" is a sentiment expressed by many individuals. "I treat everyone the same, regardless of race" is another common refrain. Some people claim that they don't "see color." A large percentage of White Americans are in a state of denial about their own racial biases and about the ways that racial bias can lead to discriminatory behavior. If people believe that they harbor no stereotypes or prejudice, they are unlikely to participate in efforts to reduce those attitudes and beliefs. For example, when we encourage individuals to participate in Healing Racism Seminars we often encounter responses like: "This sounds like a worthwhile program but it's not anything that I would need...race just isn't an issue for me."

Many research studies have explored the phenomenon of "implicit (unconscious) bias" (Kirwan Institute, 2015). These studies have found that a high percentage of White people who believe they are free of prejudice display implicit bias, leading to discriminatory behavior, in a variety of situations. For example, in a study of medical decision-making (Green et al., 2007), researchers asked emergency room and internal medicine doctors (who were mostly White) to diagnose and treat a hypothetical patient with symptoms suggesting an acute heart attack. For half of the doctors, the patient was pictured as Black; for the other half the patient was pictured as White. Before reading about the hypothetical patient, all of the doctors completed a computerized test for Implicit Bias.

The results showed a clear relationship between implicit bias and treatment recommendations. The greater the degree of implicit bias, the more likely were the doctors to offer the medically preferred treatment (thrombolysis) to a White patient than to a Black patient. These doctors were not overtly prejudiced. They believed they treated everyone the same, regardless of race. The results of the study demonstrated that, despite their conscious beliefs, they harbored implicit bias in favor of White people and those biases affected their medical decision-making.

In another study, this one of legal decision-making (Levinson, Cai, & Young, 2010), investigators found that a group of jury-eligible undergraduate and graduate students, ages 18 to 40, White and Asian-American, demonstrated implicit associations between the words "Black" and "Unpleasant" and "Black" and "Guilty." They also found that when presented with ambiguous evidence, those individuals with stronger associations between Black and Unpleasant and Black and Guilty were more likely to find that the evidence was indicative of guilt.

These, and other, studies indicate that many White people who believe they are free of racial prejudice harbor unconscious negative bias toward African-Americans, and this bias has impact on their thoughts and behavior. Finding a way to break through the barrier of denial so that implicit bias can be addressed is a major challenge.

Expectation of Racial Prejudice

People of color, for understandable reasons, often expect that White people will be prejudiced against them and will react to them in discriminatory ways (Shelton, Richeson, & Salvatore, 2005). Research studies have demonstrated that there are different degrees of this expectation and that these differences in expectations can lead to differences in emotional and behavioral reactions.

In one study (Mendoza-Denton, Downey, Purdie, Davis, & Pietrzak, 2002), African-American college students entering a predominantly White college were evaluated for "race-based rejection sensitivity." The students completed a questionnaire that asked them to answer two questions about a variety of situations they might encounter (e.g., shopping in a store, being asked a question by a professor, eating in a restaurant, being stopped by a police officer, etc.). One question asked them to rate, on a 6-point scale ranging from *very unlikely to very likely*, their expectation that someone they encounter in each of these situations would be rejecting toward them based on their race/ethnicity (e.g.: "Imagine you have just finished shopping and you are leaving the store carrying several bags. It's closing time and several people are filing out of the store at once. Suddenly, the alarm begins to sound and a security guard comes over to investigate. Would you expect the guard to stop you because of your race/ethnicity?"). The other question asked them to rate, on a 6-point scale ranging from *very unconcerned to very concerned*, how concerned or anxious they would be about being on the receiving end of rejection based on their race/ethnicity. The scores on these two questions were combined to produce a measure of *race-based rejection sensitivity*.

The students filled out these questionnaires, along with a variety of others, during orientation week. They then completed other questionnaires, focused on their emotional reactions to encounters with their professors and fellow students, every day for 21 days. At the end of the academic year, the students filled out a questionnaire that asked them to give the names of up to 10 new friends they had made over their first year of college. They then were asked to give the age, gender, and race of each friend. In addition, students answered questions about how much trust and positive emotion they felt about the university and about extracurricular groups on campus. They also answered questions about how comfortable they would be in approaching their professors or teaching assistants for help with an academic problem (these questions were also answered at the end of their second year).

The results of this study indicated that African-American students who entered college with a high degree of race-based rejection sensitivity, reported: (1) More frequent experiences of race-based negativity during their first three weeks of college and a stronger sense of alienation and rejection following such race-based negative experiences; (2) Fewer White friends at the end of their first year of college and a more negative attitude toward the university; and (3) At the end of their second year, greater resistance to seeking academic help from their professors and teaching assistants.

This study demonstrates that a high degree of race-based rejection sensitivity can be an obstacle to interracial interactions. If a person of color has a high expectation of being rejected by White people, and has a high degree of concern about being on the receiving end of such rejection, he or she is likely to avoid or minimize interacting with White people, including those who indicate a desire to participate in bridge-building initiatives. It has been said that "people see what they're looking for." If life experiences and the warnings of family and friends have cautioned a young Black person about the widespread existence of prejudice and discrimination among White people, that person is likely to be hypervigilant among members of that group and to interpret their words and behaviors through that lens.

Strategies for Overcoming Perceptual Obstacles to Engagement

Perceptual obstacles to engagement can be addressed in a variety of ways. One approach is through public presentations and forums. People who would not be willing to commit to participating in an ongoing diversity initiative may be willing to attend a one-time presentation or forum about race relations, especially if those presentations or forums are sponsored by an organization that individuals already feel a part of—their church, the local community college, their workplace, or a service organization (Lions, Elks, Kiwanis, etc.). As a result of attending such an event, perceptions can begin to shift and resistances to participating in an ongoing initiative can be reduced. For example, the forums conducted by the Race Relations Council at Lake Michigan College have focused on racial inequality in education, employment, health care, and the criminal justice system. Many of the White people who attend these forums are hearing about these racial disparities for the first time. Their perception is affected by this new information. Many of the racial minority attendees have never been to a program about racial inequality in which half the panel and half the audience is White. Their perceptions are affected by this new experience.

At the end of these forums, participants are asked to leave their contact information if they would like to learn more about the Race Relations Council. They are also asked to indicate whether they would like to participate in another forum about race relations. Many people, from different racial backgrounds, ask for additional information about the organization. Most of these people sign up to attend one or more additional forums. Some become members of the Council and participate in a variety of racial justice initiatives. The people who attend the Race Relations Council forums don't change all of their perceptions about race, but they do change some of them. And, their resistance to engaging in constructive dialogue across racial lines is reduced.

Another approach is through observing positive interracial collaborations. When the All God's Children Choir performs, audience members experience children and adults from different racial groups working together in warm, friendly, collaborative ways. At the annual Calling All Colors picnic, family members experience their children interacting enthusiastically with children from different racial backgrounds. They also see diverse staff and board members working together with warmth and ease to serve as hosts for the event. In each of these instances, observing positive interracial interactions has inspired adults who had previously avoided getting involved in any diversity initiatives to step forward and begin to participate, either by signing up their children or by offering to participate themselves. Observing positive interracial interactions is a powerful way to reduce resistances to building bridges.

Emotional Obstacles

A variety of emotions can interfere with the bridge building process. In our experience, the primary emotions that trigger resistance in White people are anxiety, anger and guilt. For people of color, we've learned that resistance is often fueled by anxiety, anger, mistrust and hope-lessness. Though there are certainly exceptions, the following general observations have emerged from multiple experiences over the past twenty-five years of working on bridge-building initiatives.

White People

Anxiety is a major obstacle to bridge building efforts. It is not uncommon for individuals to feel some anxiety when they find themselves in any unfamiliar situation. They often question what they will encounter and whether or not they will be adequately prepared to deal with the situation. Generations of segregation and longstanding stereotypes have made equal-status interracial contact "unfamiliar" to both White and Black Americans. As Dr. Martin Luther King taught us: "We fear each other because we don't know each other; we don't know each other because we are so often separated from each other." (King, 1958).

Well-intentioned White people are often afraid to engage with people of color for fear that they might "say something wrong" and trigger an angry reaction (Richeson & Shelton, 2007). This is not a completely irrational fear, since individuals who have experienced prejudice and discrimination often harbor resentment and anger toward members of the "dominant" group. In our experience, however, while individuals from racial minority groups do react to unintended hurtful remarks, they often express appreciation when they observe willingness on the part of the White participant to critically examine his or her own words, attitudes, and behaviors. For example, in the early days of the Race Relations Council, the group was discussing the differences between the phrases "Colored People" and "People of Color." One of the authors (L.F.) said: "I don't understand why African-Americans are O.K. with "People of Color" but not with "Colored People." Allene, an African-American woman from Benton Harbor, replied, with some frustration in her voice: "It's because 'People of Color' puts people before color." I immediately recognized why this mattered, and felt embarrassed that I had raised the question. Allene appreciated my willingness to learn from her, and the discussion continued in a positive way. Over the next twenty years in the Race Relations Council, there have been other temporarily uncomfortable moments that have resulted in personal growth and strengthening of our bonds of friendship and group identity.

Another form of anxiety that many White people experience is the fear of being accused of having "White Privilege" (Collins, 2018). Many individuals strongly resist the idea of White privilege. They respond with such sentiments as: "I grew up in a poor family, I have never been privileged"; "I'm not privileged, I've worked hard for everything I have"; "If you're willing to put out the effort, everybody has an equal chance to succeed—this privilege thing is just an excuse."

These sentiments ignore the reality that White people have benefitted from hundreds of years of racial discrimination, and that those benefits continue to impact our lives today. When people of color are denied equal access to education, employment, and housing, White people have greater access to these ladders of success. When White people drive a car, they don't have to worry about being pulled over for "driving while Black." When White people go into a store to shop, they are not going to be followed by a store employee who suspects, solely on the basis of skin color, that they are likely to steal something from the store. When White people apply to rent an apartment they don't have to worry that their application won't be fairly reviewed because of the color of their skin. A significant body of research substantiates the existence of these and many other forms of everyday discrimination (Richeson, 2018).

White privilege was evident in our area in the following example. A Black professional woman, her young children in the back seat of her car, stopped for gas at a local station. After filling her tank, she realized that she had left her wallet and credit cards at home. With some embarrassment, she explained her dilemma and offered to pay with a check. The station owner shouted: "I don't take any checks! You should have made sure you had the money before you filled your tank." He continued his angry tirade and threatened to call the police. The children began to cry while their mother called her husband, who rushed to the scene to pay the hostile owner. Days later, after hearing about this incident, a White teacher at a local high school decided to run an "experiment." She went to the same gas station, filled her tank, expressed dismay that she had forgotten her wallet, and offered to pay with a check. In dramatic contrast to the owner's reaction to the Black woman, he calmly reassured the White woman that this is "no problem" and he graciously accepted her check.

Resistance to the idea of White privilege can be an obstacle to participation in racial diversity initiatives. Some people who are genuinely concerned about the racial divide resist taking active steps to build bridges because they are afraid that they will encounter resentment from those who feel discriminated against and they will be "accused" of having White privilege. Their fear stops them from "sticking their necks out" and interacting with people from different racial backgrounds.

Anger. Some White people resist engaging with minorities because they are angry about being "blamed" for racial problems. "I didn't own slaves, I didn't discriminate, so why am I being blamed for this problem?" In general, individuals want to be perceived as "a good person," not someone who harbors unfair and unkind thoughts and feelings and/or demonstrates hurtful behaviors. To recognize your own role in participating in or benefitting from systemic racism makes it difficult for many people to hold onto their positive view of themselves in the world. They feel anxious, angry, and uncomfortable and push back by "blaming the victim." In work-related "diversity training" experiences, White participants may get angry at the facilitator if he or she suggests that there may be some element of racial bias in that person's reactions to their fellow employees (DiAngelo, 2018).

Other White people are angry and resentful because they believe that affirmative action policies have discriminated against the "majority group"—their group. In a 2017 poll (Struyk, 2017), a high percentage of White people (57%) said that they believe discrimination against Whites is as big a problem as discrimination against Blacks and other racial minorities. A White student in our course went one step further, exclaiming that: "White people are the most discriminated against group in America." Many opponents of affirmative action programs echo our student's sentiments.

Guilt

Another emotion that gets in the way of racial collaboration is guilt. Many White people experience this emotion, with or without conscious awareness. Those who are aware of their vulnerability to feeling guilt often avoid situations that might trigger this troubling emotion. For example, when the authors have invited White community members to attend Healing Racism seminars, we often have encountered these types of reactions: "I don't like to dwell on the past...it makes me feel guilty...and I wasn't even there."; "No thanks! I heard they show films of slaves being beaten and lynchings—even videos of discrimination and violence going on today. I don't need to participate in something that makes me feel guilty and depressed."

Learning about past and present racial injustice frequently triggers guilt in White people who are capable of empathy. In order to avoid these painful feelings, many avoid educational opportunities, as well as opportunities for meaningful dialogue with people of color.

People of Color

Anxiety

As with White people, anxiety is also an obstacle to engagement for people of color. Research studies have documented that African-American individuals often experience anxiety about being on the receiving end of prejudice if they interact with White people (Richeson & Shelton, 2007). This anxiety stimulates avoidance behavior; rather than risk experiencing a prejudiced reaction, it is safer to just avoid the interaction altogether.

Another type of anxiety experienced by some Black individuals is *fear of being accused of "acting White."* Research studies have documented the fact that being accused of "acting White" is a common experience for many African-American children, adolescents, and adults (Davis, Stadulis, & Neal-Barnett, 2018). This accusation can be emotionally damaging, especially for individuals with fragile self-esteem. In some instances it can be experienced as a form of emotional bullying (Davis, 2016).

Researcher Angela Neal-Barnett and her colleagues have developed a scale to measure the experience of being accused of "acting White" (Neal-Barnett, Stadulis, Singer, Murray, & Demmings, 2009; Davis, 2016). This scale contains a variety of items that assess different aspects of the accusation and asks how often the individual experiences each of these accusations, ranging from "never" to "almost all of the time." Included among the items are:

- Listening to "White" music
- Sitting at the lunch table with different races
- Being friends with people of different races
- Engaging in activities that are not regarded as "Black" activities

In our outreach efforts, some African-American individuals have said that talking about racial issues is a "White thing; Black people don't sit around talking about this stuff." For these people, and others who harbor similar reactions, the thought of engaging in a racial diversity initiative can trigger anxiety about being accused of "acting White." This anxiety can significantly inhibit participation in such initiatives.

Anger

Many people of color have expressed frustration and anger about racial prejudice and discrimination for a very long time. From slavery to Jim Crow segregation to modern forms of racial bias, minorities have suffered the effects of institutional racism. Numerous research studies have documented the presence of racial discrimination in the justice system, the health care system, in education, housing, and employment (Richeson, 2018). Frustration and anger are inevitable emotional reactions to such injustice.

Historically, expressing frustration and anger could bring on very negative consequences; beatings, whippings, and sometimes death by lynching. In contemporary times, the expression of these emotions could mean suspension from school, the loss of a job, or a violent response by a police officer. It is understandable then that an invitation to engage in dialogue around racial issues would be met with a great deal of skepticism and resistance. It is a rare occurrence in the lives of people of color that their expression of anger and frustration has been met with acceptance, acknowledgement, and a deepening level of empathy and understanding.

Mistrust

Mistrust is a major problem in attempts to build bridges across the racial divide. Many people of color have expressed significant mistrust toward White people (Smith, 2010), including mistrust about White people's ability to hear and care about the feelings of people of color. Like our Project Unity friend Bob, they have been repeatedly exposed to variations on the theme of: "Don't trust Whitey." These warnings from family and friends were most often based on painful life experiences and were issued in an attempt to protect the next generation and keep them safe from harm.

Exploitative and discriminatory behaviors from White people in their own lives reinforce the messages of childhood. When social media and news reports document racial injustice in a variety of contexts, the belief that "White people cannot be trusted" is fortified and expanded upon. This barrier to entering into a shared experience is formidable but, in our experience, not insurmountable.

Hopelessness and Despair

Other feelings that fuel resistance by people of color are hopelessness and despair. Research studies (Nyborg & Curry, 2003; Vineset al., 2006) provide a body of data indicating that systemic racism, with generations struggling under the shadow of prejudice and discrimination, has generated a relatively high prevalence of these emotions. There is a widespread feeling, especially among African-Americans, that "the system is rigged against me." One example: When a talented Black high school student in our area was offered an opportunity for technical training on a new product by a local manufacturer, he refused the invitation, saying: "I don't want to become just another cog in the White man's machine." There was certainly frustration and anger in his response, but also a sense of hopelessness, a belief that none of his efforts would allow him to move out of poverty and into a "successful" life. Hopelessness breeds apathy and despair. When individuals are experiencing these emotions, it is difficult to engage them in efforts toward social change.

Strategies for Overcoming Emotional Obstacles to Engagement

We know that separation and alienation provide a breeding ground for the development of stereotypes, prejudice, and emotional resistance to interracial engagement. Our first task in overcoming this resistance is to venture into White and non-White communities and begin to develop trust as credible, caring individuals. "Outsiders" are often met with suspicion and skepticism. If we want to engage individuals in bridge building activities, especially in highly segregated areas, we must be willing to respectfully interface with community organizations and community leaders and establish ourselves as "safe" and "trustworthy."

Forming alliances with those who have established trust and regard in their communities—pastors, block club presidents, leaders of service organizations, educators, etc.—can open doors and allow for some transfer of credibility. In our beginning efforts to form the All God's Children Choir, we often heard people say: "If our pastor thinks you're OK then I'll give your choir a try." In the early days of Calling All Colors, we heard comments like: "If our school principal signed onto Calling All Colors, it must be a good program." Anxiety and mistrust begin to dissipate with the endorsement of trusted individuals and organizations.

Another helpful approach is to identify an activity that is already valued in and of itself by individuals from different racial backgrounds–singing, dancing, athletics, etc. Bringing people together around a shared interest is often an effective strategy for reducing emotional resistance.

Identifying a safe space in which people can gather and hear about the initiative is a valuable step in reducing resistance. In choosing the location for this initial meeting, it is important to become knowledgeable about the history of the area, the feelings attached to certain locations, and what is most likely to be perceived as "race neutral" territory. For example, the initial meeting that led to the creation of the Race Relations

Council took place at Lake Michigan College, one of the very few locations in this highly segregated area where White and non-White individuals regularly interact. People from both sides of the river were willing to meet at the college, even though they had a great deal of anxiety about participating in an interracial initiative. Familiarity with the college quieted some of the anxiety—people saw this location as a "safe space."

Anxiety can also be reduced by talking about the initiative in ways that are likely to be reassuring to all racial groups. We need to be clear that our initiative is not about fault finding, but rather it is about dispelling stereotypes, deepening mutual understanding, and finding common ground. Describing the format of the program and noting the presence of trained adult coordinators and facilitators helps dissipate some of the apprehension. For example, in the Calling All Colors program parents, teachers, and administrators are reassured by the highly structured approach and the presence of well-trained group facilitators. In Healing Racism, there are clear guidelines for sharing experiences, thoughts, and feelings with the group. The presence of guidelines and boundaries, enforced by skilled leaders, can be very helpful in overcoming some of the emotional obstacles to engagement.

Another way to reduce anxiety is to highlight aspects of the initiative that bring people together in ways that respect everyone's "home base." For example, when approaching parents about the possibility of their child or children joining the All God's Children choir, we make the point that this choir rehearses on both sides of the river so that everyone can learn to feel at home in every community.

Resistance born out of hopelessness can be countered, in part, by sharing "success stories" from the current, or previous, initiatives. We might discuss, for example, the accomplishments of the Race Relations Council in the areas of housing, education, health, and criminal justice. We might also cite the openness, spontaneity, and friendships that have developed among the Council members as a result of our collaboration on a series of racial justice projects.

Modeling of positive interracial interactions is a powerful means for reducing anxiety, anger, and hopelessness. Viewing the warm collaboration between the children and adults in the All God's Children Choir, or the comfortable camaraderie of the Race Relations Council and Calling All

Colors board members as we host our annual fun(d)raiser, observers find it easier to believe that rigid boundaries could be reduced, trust could be established, and we could all be together in more harmonious ways.

Staying Engaged: Sustaining Involvement Once the Process Is Underway

Once an interracial initiative has begun, the organizers need to continue to be mindful of those differences in perception and those problematic emotions that spurred resistance at the outset. The same challenges will persist to some degree during the initiative itself and it is the organizers' response to these challenges that will determine the longevity and effectiveness of the process. For example, during one of the early sessions of our Healing Racism seminar the meeting began with a powerful video providing a disturbing look at our nation's racial history. Several Black participants expressed outrage; several White participants expressed sadness, shame, and guilt. The room was heavy with emotions most people want to avoid. Had those emotions been left "untended," it is likely that some group members would not have returned for subsequent sessions. The coordinators' response, however, was to move directly into the "active listening" exercise so that each person was allowed a limited block of time to express their feelings without judgment, limitation, or feedback from their listening partner. The power of going on record, of being heard, and then offering the "other" the same respect by listening to his or her expression of emotion, relieved much of the tension and deepened the bond of understanding between the participants. Making your way through a difficult experience together cultivates a "we feeling" within the group and furthers the goals of the bridge-building initiative.

With initiatives that involve children, like Calling All Colors, adult leaders need to monitor interactions, recognizing that an interracial grouping is unfamiliar in highly segregated communities. Children will understandably carry the stereotypes learned from their families and neighborhoods into the situation and these judgments can trigger anxiety, misinterpretation, and defensiveness. By assigning "buddies" and directing them into playful, collaborative tasks, facilitators can counter stereotypes, reduce feelings of alienation, and prompt recognition of common ground. Children, like adults, will want to return to an experience that they find gratifying. Continuity of engagement is far more likely when discomfort is reduced and positive experiences are increased.

In developing strategies for overcoming obstacles and maintaining engagement, we repeatedly return to the basic guidelines offered by Intergroup Contact Theory: Personal connection, Equal Status, Shared Goals, Cooperative interaction, Repeated contact over time, Modeling, Sanction from relevant authorities, and Support for the development of friendships. In our experience, participants most often "drop out" of interracial initiatives when one or more of these guidelines are disregarded or compromised. For example, if all leadership roles are occupied by individuals from the same racial background, the condition of equal status is not heeded and feelings of resentment are likely to emerge. If the structure does not promote shared goals and cooperative interaction, a shared group identity is not likely to develop and participants are more likely to withdraw from the initiative. If anger is not channeled into constructive dialogue, anxiety will escalate and participants will avoid uncomfortable discussions in the future. Without repeated contact over time, gains in building bridges will be severely limited.

Fortunately, we have the Contact Theory guidelines at our disposal. Armed with these tools, and knowledge of the unique characteristics of each community, we can engage a diverse group of participants who will be able to "ride out" difficult moments in the process and make a significant contribution to building bridges across the racial divide.

References

Collins, C. (2018). What is white privilege, really? *Teaching Tolerance, Issue 60*, www.tolerance.org

Craig, M. A., & Richeson, J. A. (2014). On the precipice of a "majority-minority" America: Perceived status threat from the racial demographic shift affects White Americans' political ideology. *Psychological Science, 25*(6), 1189–1197.

Davis, M. (2016). *Assessing the effects of the acting White accusation: Social anxiety and bullying victimization*. (Dissertation), Kent State University, Ohio. etd.ohiolink.edu.

Davis, M., Stadulis, R., & Neal-Barnett, A. (2018). Assessing the effects of the acting White accusation among Black girls: Social anxiety and bullying victimization. *Journal of the National Medical Association, 110*(1), 23–28.

DiAngelo, R. (2018). *White fragility: Why it's so hard for White people to talk about racism.* Boston, MA: Beacon Press.

Green, A. R., Carney, D. R., Pallin, D. J., Ngo, L. H., Raymond, K. L., Iezzoni, L. I., & Banaji, M. R. (2007). Implicit bias among physicians and its prediction of thrombolysis decisions for black and white patients. *Journal of General Internal Medicine, 22*(9), 1231–1238.

King, M. L. (1958). Advice for living. *Ebony, 13*(7), 112.

Kirwan Institute. (2015). *Understanding implicit bias.* Kirwan Institute for the Study of Race and Ethnicity. kirwaninstitute.osu.edu/

Knowles, E. D., Lowery, B. S., Chow, R. M., & Unzueta, M. M. (2014). Deny, distance, or dismantle? How White Americans manage a privileged identity. *Perspectives in Psychological Science, 9*(6), 594–609.

Levinson, J. D., Cai, H., & Young, D. (2010). Guilty by implicit racial bias: The guilty/not guilty Implicit Association Test. *Ohio State Journal of Criminal Law, 8,* 187–208.

Mendoza-Denton, R., Downey, G., Purdie, V., J., Davis, A. & Pietrzak, J. (2002). Sensitivity to status-based rejection: Implications for African American students' college experience. *Journal of Personality and Social Psychology, 83*(4), 896–918.

Neal-Barnett, A., Staduli, R., Singer, N., Murray, M., & Demmings, J. (2009). Assessing the effects of experiencing the acting white accusation. *The Urban Review, 42*(2), 102–122.

Nyborg, V. M., & Curry, J. F. (2003). The impact of perceived racism: Psychological symptoms among African American boys. *Journal of Clinical Child and Adolescent Psychology, 32*(2), 258–266.

Richeson, J. A. (2018). The psychology of racism: An introduction to the special issue. *Current Directions in Psychological Science, 27*(3), 148–149.

Richeson, J. A., & Shelton, J. N. (2007). Negotiating interracial interactions: Costs, consequences, and possibilities. *Current Directions in Psychological Science, 16*(6), 316–320.

Shelton, J. N., Richeson, J. A., & Salvatore, J. (2005). Expecting to be the target of prejudice: Implications for interethnic interactions. *Personality and Social Psychology Bulletin, 31*(9), 1189–1202.

Sidanius, J., Cotterill, S., Sheehy-Skeffington, J., Kteily, N., & Carvacho, H. (2016). Social dominance theory: Explorations in the psychology of oppression. In C. G. Sibley & F. K. Barlow (Eds), *The Cambridge handbook of the psychology of prejudice* (149–187). Cambridge: Cambridge University Press.

Smith, S. (2010). Race and trust. *Annual Review of Sociology, 36,* 453–475.

Struyk, R. (2017, August 18). *Blacks and whites see racism in the United States very, very differently.* CNN.com

Vines, A. I., Baird, D. D., McNeilly, M., Hertz-Picciotto, I., Light, K. C., & Steven, J. (2006). Social correlates of the chronic stress of perceived racism among black women. *Ethnicity & Disease, 16*(1), 101–107.

Chapter 10

Guidelines for Moving Forward

In previous chapters, we have reviewed the extensive research literature on the many and varied benefits of positive interracial contact. We have presented detailed examples of effective diversity initiatives for children, teens, college students, and adults. We have delineated a variety of strategies that parents and teachers can use to reduce implicit and explicit racial bias. We have discussed perceptual and emotional resistances to becoming involved in bridge-building initiatives, and have presented a variety of strategies for overcoming these resistances.

In this, our final chapter, we build on the material we have previously presented to describe specific guidelines for creating and maintaining effective racial diversity initiatives. Each guideline is illustrated with examples from one or more of the initiatives we have discussed in earlier chapters.

Guideline #1: Take a Broad and Deep Look at the Community You Are Interested in Serving. What Is the Current State of Race Relations in That Community? What Is Its History? How Do Varied Groups Look at the Race Relations "Problems" in Their Community?

Before any diversity initiative is fully conceptualized and launched, it is important to develop a rich understanding of the community that you're dealing with. The importance of *listening* to community members, inviting them to share the history of the area and their own experiences, cannot be overstated. Inquiring about previous efforts at improving race relations, the ways in which they succeeded and the challenges they faced, is also critically important. Respectful inquiry is, in and of itself, an exercise in bridge building. If community members and organizations do not experience you as sincere, respectful, and trustworthy, you are likely to run into multiple roadblocks. "Doing your homework" indicates that you value the members of the community and their input. They will be more likely to become stakeholders in the initiative, to open doors to other participants and resources, and to become invested in the outcome.

Illustrative Examples

Project Unity was initiated by two mothers, Cheryl Capps and Karin Grimes—one Black, one White—living in the racially integrated community of Oak Park, Illinois. These mothers were aware of Oak Park's history of taking strong action to resist "White flight" as families of color began moving into the community. They were also aware that it takes more than geographic proximity to create true racial diversity.

Cheryl and Karin were troubled by their observation that while children in Oak Park often developed diverse friendship groups in elementary school, by the time they reached high school their friendship groups were racially homogeneous. At a parent-student forum where this issue was discussed, the students pointed out that their parents didn't interact much across racial lines either. Cheryl and Karin were convinced that this was a major part of the problem.

The two women broadened their inquiry to include other individuals and groups in the community. They found out that many other families shared their concern and saw this as a problem they wished could be corrected.

Cheryl and Karin realized that to create a truly integrated community there was a need for personal interactions. Their vision was that if people could meet on a regular basis, in each other's homes, racial barriers could be reduced and mutual understanding and trust could be developed. They knew that this process would not always go smoothly, but they also knew that the people who would volunteer to participate in this initiative would be committed to the project and would do all they could to make it work.

Race Relations Council and Twin Cities Together

In stark contrast to Oak Park, Illinois, Southwest Michigan is one of the most racially segregated regions in the country. When we first moved to this area more than twenty years ago, we were surprised and dismayed to discover the degree of racial segregation and racial inequality that existed between the "twin cities" of Benton Harbor and St. Joseph, two towns separated only by a river. In exploring the history of the area, we discovered that the current state of affairs had evolved over time (Butzbaugh, 2003). In the 1940's, Benton Harbor was a predominantly White town, with year-round residents and a bustling tourist trade. That began to change as African-Americans migrated north looking for factory work and looking to escape the racial discrimination and violence of the south. By 1960, the non-White population of Benton Harbor was about 35%. Over time, as more Black people moved in, more White people moved out. The pattern of "White flight" that was occurring in many parts of the country took hold in Southwest Michigan. During the 1960s and 1970s, many White people moved into the surrounding, predominantly White, communities. As they did so, many businesses and civic institutions, like the YMCA, moved with them. The major employer in Benton Harbor moved many of its factories out of state and many Benton Harbor line workers found themselves out of work. Over time, Benton Harbor became a predominantly Black, and economically depressed, community. St. Joseph, which had initially been a smaller and less prosperous town than Benton Harbor, began to grow and to become more prosperous. By the time we moved to the area in 1997, the pattern of racial segregation and racial inequality was well established. The differences between the two communities were startling. Knowledge of the history was critical in determining what forms of outreach might be successful.

Residents of Benton Harbor and St. Joseph were certainly aware of the current discrepancies, but the publication in 1998 of Alex Kotlowitz's book *The Other Side of the River* brought them to national attention. The media response to this book prompted a number of local residents to come together in an effort to build bridges between these communities and to take steps to reduce the inequality, hostility, and mistrust that had developed over time. Those of us who participated in the creation of those initial bridge-building efforts knew that people in both communities were wary of such initiatives. Many Benton Harbor residents had grown up hearing admonitions to not trust White people. They had heard repeatedly that White people had exploited Blacks and abandoned their community. Many St. Joseph residents had grown up being fearful of Benton Harbor residents, who had been stereotypically portrayed as irresponsible, impulsive and violent. It became clear that bringing individuals from these two communities together to identify specific problems and propose and implement specific solutions was not going to be easy. Without insight into prevailing attitudes and beliefs, it would have been impossible.

Despite the obstacles, two racially diverse groups of people did come together to begin planning bridge-building initiatives. Some of us participated in both of these groups. One group proposed organizing a Race Relations Council. The other group, which named itself "Twin Cities Together," proposed starting a Calling All Colors program. Those of us who planned these initiatives knew the history of the area and the level of animosity that had grown up over the years, but we were determined to work together to reduce hostility, mistrust, and inequality in our community.

Guideline #2: Generate a Clear Idea About the Kind of Initiative You Want to Create, Why You Think This Type of Initiative Is Needed, and What You Hope It Will Accomplish

Well-intentioned individuals and groups are often aware of race-related problems in their area and feel a responsibility to "do something" to make things better. If, however, these intentions remain vague and un-tethered, the problems are likely to remain unsolved. Preliminary work on developing a clear vision is important before attempting to engage others in any diversity initiative. Idealized goals without a clear pathway to achievement may offer temporary encouragement but will fail to engage participants over time.

The structure of the initiative, though open to modification, must be provided at the outset: "This is the problem we're addressing. These are the ways we'll tackle it. These are the goals we hope to achieve." With that kind of clarity, a new diversity initiative is far more likely to attract and sustain active participation,

Illustrative Examples

The Race Relations Council was formed as a project-oriented initiative, focused on a variety of areas in which racial inequality was very much in evidence. Those of us who organized the Council envisioned divid-ing into a series of sub-groups, focused on specific areas of concern—education, employment, housing, criminal justice, health care, social attitudes and behavior. We hoped to devise one or more projects that would shed light on inequality in each of these areas, and move the community forward toward equal opportunity for all. We also hoped that by working together on these projects we would come to know one another as individuals rather than stereotypes and that we could provide a model for the community of racial bridge building.

Calling All Colors (CAC) was originally created at Coastal Caro-lina University as a one-day event in which children from different racial backgrounds came together and shared engaging activities designed to reduce stereotypes and mistrust. When the Twin Cities Together group was discussing what initiatives might be good to start in Southwest Michigan, a few individuals who knew of the Coastal Carolina initiative—Mary and George Wilson, Andy Sawyer, and Nita Nicholie—urged the group to embrace the Calling All Colors concept.

Initially, we began with a once a year format based on the original design. After a few years, we realized that although the children enjoyed the experience, once a year was not enough to make a significant difference in how they viewed the children from "the other side of the river." More contact was needed, and it had to be carefully structured. We divided into grade levels, expanded the program to two mornings for each class during the school year, and added ongoing pen pal exchanges and a picnic for the children and their families in the late spring. Our hope was that as the children experienced one another while participating together in a variety of engaging diversity education modules, the barriers would weaken, they would discover that they were more alike than different, and friendships would begin to develop. We also hoped that the end-of-year picnic would provide an opportunity for the parents of the CAC participants to experience their children interacting enthusiastically with children from other backgrounds, and that the parents themselves might develop somewhat greater ease interacting across racial lines in this relaxed, informal social setting.

Guideline #3: Decide How the Initiative Will Meet the Conditions of Intergroup Contact Theory

In previous chapters we have discussed the enduring relevance of Intergroup Contact Theory as a vehicle for understanding the interactions between diverse individuals and groups. The conditions described by Gordon Allport as necessary for the reduction of stereotypes and prejudice continue to serve as valuable guides in developing, executing, and maintaining diversity initiatives. If we fail to provide opportunities for personal interaction, equal status, shared goals, and cooperation rather than competition, our efforts will be unsuccessful. Similarly, we need to make positive connections with respected authorities in the community. Ensuring that these conditions are adhered to is important in achieving the best possible outcome.

Personal Interaction

When we began planning for the *All God's Children Community Choir,* we knew that we wanted to create as many opportunities for personal interaction as possible—interaction between the choir members, between the parents and, in some instances, between the grandparents. For that reason our plans included a shared meal at the end of each rehearsal, a meal in which families would contribute a dish or help with the preparation, serving, or clean-up. We envisioned this post-rehearsal time as an opportunity for choir members and their families to share stories, discover common interests, celebrate special occasions, and enjoy one another's company. We were hopeful that the personal interactions that occurred during this meal-sharing time would stimulate other forms of personal interaction outside of the structure of rehearsals and performances—experiences like play dates, birthday parties, attending school or community events in which choir members had featured roles, etc.

Calling All Colors was expanded from one annual event to a series of experiences during the school year because we wanted to increase the opportunities for personal interactions between the students. We also wanted to add small group modules and two-person "buddy" activities for the same reason. Pen pal exchanges were designed to provide an additional form of contact, as was the end-of-the year picnic. The program's expansion included students from first, second, third, and fourth grades so that there would be an accumulation of contacts during the elementary school years.

Equal Status

When we first had the idea of creating the *All God's Children Choir* we knew we wanted to have a diverse group of choir directors. We thought that by reaching out to a Black and a White pastor who had expressed an interest in racial reconciliation we might be able to not only receive assistance in recruiting choir members, but also receive help in recruiting the youth choir directors from the pastors' churches to collaborate with us in directing the new community choir. We knew it would be important for the children from all racial groups to see people who looked like them in leadership roles.

Furthering the principle of equal status, we decided at the outset to hold our rehearsals in a variety of different communities. We wanted to send a clear message that every community has value and that all of us could come to feel "at home" in every community. We were hoping that choir members and their families would feel proud to "host" the choir at their church, library, or community center and that the children and their families would become comfortable crossing the bridge that led to "the other side of the river."

We were also conscious of ensuring equal status by distributing solo opportunities to children from all racial groups. We wanted everyone to have equal access to "special parts."

The vision for *Calling All Colors* also called for a diverse leadership team. When the children initially assembled in a large group we wanted them to see facilitators that represented the diversity of the participants. In the small groups, our goal was to have two facilitators, one White and one non-White. We have not always been able to make this happen, but we have always tried to come as close to that goal as possible.

In our training sessions, we planned to work with facilitators to help them be mindful of promoting equal status participation. In the large group experience, we wanted them to have a clear commitment to selecting students from diverse groups as volunteers. In the small groups, we wanted them to make sure that students from all racial backgrounds had an equal opportunity to participate in every activity and discussion.

Shared Goals and Cooperative Interaction

Project Unity was formed to promote personal interactions between members of different racial groups. The organizers planned to begin the initiative by placing an ad in the local paper announcing the formation and goals of the group and inviting everyone who shared those goals to participate. Their vision was that those who expressed interest in the project would agree to meet once a month in each other's homes for discussions about race-related issues. They imagined an informal structure, with the host individual or couple loosely coordinating the discussion. Topics would be brought up by members of the group. Everyone would make a commitment to listen carefully and empathically to one another and to respond honestly and respectfully. The group process would be guided by everyone's commitment to deepening their understanding of each other's experiences and forming authentic relationships.

The Race Relations Council came together around two shared goals: improvement of race relations and reduction (ideally, elimination) of racial inequality in Southwest Michigan. We planned to work together to develop projects to promote these goals. The process we envisioned was one of collaborative brainstorming, followed by shared implementation. When we disagreed about either the plan or the implementation process we were committed to cooperative problem solving, in which everyone was free to express their opinion and the final decision would be made either by consensus or by the majority of the group. We hoped that our collaborative process would in and of itself represent movement toward our shared goals.

Sanction by Relevant Authorities

As we mentioned previously, in planning for the *All God's Children Choir*, the first step we contemplated taking was contacting two pastors, one from Benton Harbor and one from St. Joseph. The decision to contact the pastors at the outset was prompted by feedback we received from many community members, who told us that "faith leaders" were highly regarded in Southwest Michigan and that the endorsement of any project by those leaders would lend credibility and value to that project. We thought that the pastors we had chosen to approach might be helpful since they had participated in the early formation of the Race Relations Council. We also hoped that once the choir was launched support would broaden to include a variety of other community authorities—educators, business and political leaders, etc.

Calling All Colors also needed the support of relevant authorities. Because the program operates during the school day, it was critical that we engage school administrators at the outset and present a compelling argument that Calling All Colors would provide a rich learning experience and enhance life in our communities. We were hopeful that once superintendents and principals endorsed the program, teachers would be willing and able to make the investment of time and energy necessary for Calling All Colors to be successful.

We also knew we would need the support of a community organization to provide a home for the program. We initially approached the St. Joseph YWCA, which readily agreed to provide space for Calling All Colors. Over the years, other community organizations, including the Salvation Army and the Boys and Girls Club, have provided invaluable assistance, and their involvement has added credibility to the program in the community.

Guideline #4: Plan an Initial Meeting in a "Neutral" Location and Launch the Initiative

If you set up the initial meeting in a site where multiple groups feel comfortable and safe, you're off to a good start. If, on the other hand, your initial meeting takes place in a location that is historically connected with discriminatory practices or with violence, you will draw a much smaller pool of participants.

Project Unity initially met in an Oak Park church, with a reputation for its "open door" policy. Churches are often perceived as "safe spaces." The organizers shared the impetus for the Project Unity idea and talked about their hopes for the initiative. They quickly moved to engage the participants in discussions about race-related problems, allowing all who were present to share their perspective. They elicited feedback regarding their tentative plans for structuring the project and demonstrated a willingness to modify the format in light of suggestions and the consensus of the group. Launching Project Unity in this way maximized the chance for "buy-in" from the community.

The initial meeting of the *Race Relations Council* was held at Lake Michigan College, a location that is comfortable for residents of both Benton Harbor and St. Joseph. In this highly segregated region, the college is often the first place where Black and White students experience people from a different racial background. It is a truly integrated institution. The coordinator of that initial meeting was Dr. Ron Field, an African-American educator who served as the Vice President of Lake Michigan College at that time. The purpose of the meeting was to brainstorm with a diverse group of concerned community members about the issues raised in Alex Kotlowitz's book *The Other Side of the River,* to take stock of the current state of affairs in multiple arenas, and to determine an action plan for moving forward. We contemplated organizing ourselves into a Council that would include subgroups made up of individuals with certain areas of expertise and/or concern—education, housing, criminal justice, etc.

We knew we wanted this initiative to be racially diverse and to have both male and female participants. By the end of this preliminary meeting, a group of twenty people, diverse in each of these ways, had volunteered to participate in the second organizational meeting. As in our previous example, engaging those in attendance to be active participants in the early formation of the initiative was critical for a successful "launch."

Guideline #5: Process the Initial Meeting and Make Needed Adjustments

Following the initial meeting it is important to take stock of how things went, what ideas were generated, what plans were made about how to move forward, and what if any problems arose. If these questions are not examined, difficulties may arise that could have been nipped in the bud if they had been examined earlier.

Illustrative Examples

After the initial organizational gathering, *Project Unity* groups began meeting in members' homes. In the group we joined, everyone agreed that meeting in peoples' homes created an atmosphere of personal connection that was very positive; the feeling was one of neighbors getting together with neighbors in pursuit of a common goal.

As our group began to discuss how we wanted to organize our meetings, we realized that in the initial launching of Project Unity, little attention had been paid to the format of the small groups and to methods for resolving differences in individual's preferences for a particular format. While everyone in our group shared the same goals, there were clear differences in how we envisioned the group achieving these goals. Some people wanted to focus only on discussions of issues raised by group members. Others wanted to read relevant books and discuss ideas presented in the books. Some people wanted to share social experiences periodically; others did not. These differences were discussed, compromises negotiated, and tentative agreements were reached with the understanding that if at any point the group wanted to make a change in the format we could do so. Everyone agreed to meet once a month and to participate in the planned annual dinner-dance, where participants in all the groups could enjoy each other's company and plan for the future of Project Unity.

The second meeting of the Race Relations Council began with a review of the first, much larger, meeting. Everyone agreed that the first meeting had been productive and that a race relations council was definitely needed in our area. We hoped that the smaller size of the group at the second meeting would be more workable for developing action plans. While a large meeting can provide an opportunity for many issues to be identified, feelings to be aired, and possible solutions to be proposed, the smaller group was likely to be more effective at consolidating ideas and designing and implementing projects.

Based on the discussion in the first meeting, we created issue-oriented committees and agreed to focus initially on gathering information about racial attitudes and behavior in St. Joseph and Benton Harbor. We also agreed that we needed to confront an issue that had arisen between the first and second meeting. As we discussed in an earlier chapter, the Ku Klux Klan had announced that they were planning to hold a rally in St. Joseph. That announcement prompted very intense discussion among the members of the Council about how best to cope with this development. Ultimately, we opted to write a letter to the editor of the local paper stating our opposition to the Klan and urging the community to turn out in force to support a Unity Service in Benton Harbor that was being planned for the same time as the Klan rally.

We ended our second meeting by agreeing to meet once a month. One of the members of the Council offered to provide meeting space for the organization at his place of business, the local community development agency located in Benton Harbor.

Guideline #6: Implement the Initiative and Monitor Its Progress

We have learned from experience that unless an initiative moves rather quickly into an "action phase," enthusiasm will dissipate and participants are likely to lose interest. Through the years we have heard many individuals complain that there was "too much talking, not enough doing." While careful planning is critical, leaders need to move forward toward implementation and ride the wave of early excitement about new possibilities.

Participants' energy is highest in the early days of an initiative, as are their hopes and expectations. These emotions are necessary for launching, but they are not sufficient to sustain a project over time. There must be a commitment to monitor the progress of the initiative, to assess what is working well and what is not working well, and to keep a finger on the pulse of the membership. Participants need to feel that their efforts are bearing fruit. Tracking progress on established goals is important in ensuring the effectiveness of the initiative and in keeping the membership fully engaged. If it becomes clear that elements of the project are not working according to plan, adjustments may need to be made. Successful initiatives demonstrate flexibility and the capacity to modify their approach over time.

Illustrative Examples

The All God's Children Choir began practicing for its debut performance by the second half of our first gathering. The children and their families had received mixed tapes of our first song selections so they were able to "hit the ground running." Moving quickly into the action phase—in this case "being" a choir—allowed us to build on the initial excitement about the initiative.

The audience response to the choir's debut was extremely positive. In the weeks and months following the event, performance requests from the community began pouring in. It was a very exciting time! The coordinators, directors, children, and families felt valued by the community. The model of interracial harmony was having an impact.

Rehearsals were scheduled only twice a month in order to allow choir members to continue to participate in other activities that they already valued—church youth group, sports, dance, band, etc. Initially we scheduled rehearsals for Saturday afternoons, but soon discovered that there were too many competing events on that day of the week. We decided to switch to Sunday afternoon, and attendance picked up. There were, and still are, times when other activities cut into attendance at our rehearsals, but by and large Sunday afternoons have worked well. Without monitoring the ebb and flow of participation and modifying our schedule accordingly, it would have been difficult to sustain this initiative over time.

One of the choir's early performance requests came from Lake Michigan College, which holds a community-wide event every year commemorating the Dr. Martin Luther King, Jr. holiday. The college representative who contacted us said they would like the choir to perform for this event because "the All God's Children Choir is the best representation of Dr. King's dream." We enthusiastically accepted the college's invitation, and the choir has been invited back every year since that first performance. More recently, All God's Children was invited to perform in Chicago at Navy Pier on MLK day. When we explained that we had a standing commitment to perform at Lake Michigan College for their MLK day breakfast, the Chicago coordinator offered to send a tour bus to pick us up in Michigan and bring us to Navy Pier for an afternoon performance. As we reflected on the positive impact the choir was having in Southwest Michigan, we were delighted to extend our reach into the Chicago area.

Over the past nineteen years, many children, teens, and families have joined the choir. Some children began at an early age and have continued to rehearse and perform with the group through high school graduation. Others joined for a few years and then moved on.

During the life of the choir we have been touched by the development of many friendships across racial lines. Choir members have spent time at each other's homes, gone to plays and concerts, performed together at local open mics, visited each other on college campuses, and served as bridesmaids at a choir friend's wedding. We have seen how the positive contact over time between choir members from different racial groups has reduced racial barriers and promoted lasting friendships. We have appreciated the warm bonds that have developed and persisted between their families as well.

The relationships between the diverse group of choir directors have also grown and deepened through the years. From the beginning, Sandy has been one of the choir directors and Larry has been the accompanist. Hursel Cole, one of the original church youth choir directors, has been with All God's Children since its inception, now almost 20 years ago. Soon after the formation of the group, another director, Corey Hampton, came on board and has continued to be with the choir to the present day. Both Hursel and Corey have always been highly regarded as choir directors in the community and their reputation has added credibility to All God's Children. For several years a choir parent, Stephanie Ng, contributed her expertise as an ethnomusicologist, musician, and director. The most recent addition to our directing team, Hursel's daughter Kortney Moore, began as a choir member and soloist at age 10 and assumed a leadership role as a young adult. Kortney's six-year-old son has joined the ranks and now participates in the choir.

All God's Children has developed the feeling of an extended family. Celebration of life cycle events and support in times of crisis have taken us beyond our original goals. For the children, teens, families, directors, and community, All God's Children is a model of what can happen when people reach out across the racial divide and work together to build bonds of collaboration and friendship.

As we previously described, *Calling All Colors* was launched in the Benton Harbor—St. Joseph area nineteen years ago as a once-a-year activity. Diversity modules were interspersed with "just for fun" activities. Children of all ages participated together as a single group. The children had a good time, but personal interactions were limited and there wasn't much evidence of "take away" lessons regarding common ground and the breakdown of stereotypes.

When we recognized the limitations of the once-a-year structure, we created "our version" of Calling All Colors. The program was expanded to two mornings during the school year for each grade, one through four, followed by pen pal exchanges and a picnic in the late spring. Elementary school classrooms from Benton Harbor and St. Joseph were matched in order to provide an experience of racial/ethnic diversity. The schools began providing buses to bring the children to a "neutral" location—initially the YWCA in St. Joseph; currently, the Boys and Girls Club in Benton Harbor. The school administrators' willingness to take on the bus expense was enormously helpful to the program. Other than busing, there were no other costs to the schools.

From the beginning, we have been acutely aware of the need to monitor the "coming together" of these two groups, long separated not only by a river but also by an even greater psychological divide. Mistrust is obvious from the point of first contact. Students enter the program wary, hesitant, keeping their distance. As they attend the opening large group assembly, interspersed with "silly" skits designed to ease the tension yet introduce important concepts, the discomfort begins to dissipate. When student volunteers from each school slip into adult shoes and attempt to shuffle across the room we can all see how difficult it can be to truly understand the challenges of "walking in another person's shoes!"

Small group experiences and partnering with a "buddy" from the other school help to move the children into increasingly comfortable interactions. When they trace their partner's hand and identify each other's skin color as either "peanut butter, fudge, or vanilla," giggles can be heard around the room. Reading a book about the role of melanin and its connection to the equator prompts guesses about where each of our ancestors may have come from.

By the time the children leave their small groups and return for the closing assembly, we observe significant changes in their behavior toward one another. Arms draped across shoulders, animated chatter—these strangers are starting to become friends. Following up at the spring picnic, students are clearly delighted to reconnect with their Calling All Colors pals and they easily participate together in a variety of recreational activities. The parents appear more distant at first but after a short while they begin to connect with one another, sharing stories about their families and joining in with the children to sing songs and play games. By the end of the afternoon these children and their families have all participated in an integrated, light-hearted experience—an experience all too rare in Southwest Michigan.

In addition to observing the interactions between the children, the effectiveness of the program has been monitored in a variety of other ways. Teachers complete an evaluative questionnaire at the end of the year. Students fill out a brief evaluation instrument before and after their participation in the program. The results from each of these evaluation tools are carefully reviewed and have consistently been very positive. In addition, students and teachers have written testimonials about their experiences in Calling All Colors. These have also reassured us that this initiative is effectively pursuing its goals. One fourth-grader, enthusiastically reflecting on his experience, commented: "If everyone had a chance to participate in Calling All Colors, and have a buddy, Dr. King's dream could come true."

Conclusion

The theory, research, and examples highlighted throughout the book provide a roadmap for those who wish to initiate and/or participate in bridge-building activities. Our sincere hope is that *Building Bridges Across the Racial Divide* will inspire readers to consider ways in which they might use their own talents, energy, dreams, and frustrations to make a difference in the world around them. The possibilities are limitless. The "Beloved Community" is still within our reach.

Index

K

King, Jr, Martin Luther, ix, 19–20, 84, 95, 152, 176
   dream of racial equality, ix, 19, 20, 176, 179
Kinz, Anisa, 28
Kotlowitz, Alex, 20, 102, 140, 166, 173
Ku Klux Klan, confronting the, 102–103, 133, 141

L

Lake Michigan College, 76, 84, 104, 105, 136, 137, 150, 159, 173, 176
Lewis, John, x–xi

M

media and stereotype reduction, 112–113
media and stereotype reinforcement, 111
Michigan Archives Library, University of Michigan, 137
Modeling, *see* Intergroup Contact Theory, Change Processes *and* Conditions
Moore, Kortney, 177
Multicultural and Anti-Bias education, 49
   Empathy Building, 50
     Building Social-Cognitive Skills, 51
     Multicultural Curriculum, 49
     Teaching About Historical Racism, 50

N

Ng, Stephanie, 177
Nicholie, Nita, 168

O

Oak Leaves community paper, 136
Oak Park, Illinois, 36, 97, 98, 100, 135–136, 164, 165, 172

P

Perceptual Obstacles to Engagement, 145–150, 163
   Denial or Minimization of Racial Stereotypes and Prejudice, 147–148
   Expectation of Racial Prejudice, 148–150
   Perceptions of Racial Discrimination, Differences, 146–147
   resentment of White people's denial or minimization of racial discrimination, 147
Personal Interactions, *see* Intergroup Contact Theory, Conditions
planning the initial meeting, 172–173
processing the initial meeting and making needed adjustments, 173–175
Project Unity, 36, 97–101, 128, 130, 132–133, 135–136, 138, 139–140, 142–143, 164–165, 170–171, 172–173, 174
pro-social television shows, 41
Psychology of Stereotypes and Prejudice, The, x, 76–84, 127, 130, 131–132, 135, 138, 138–139, 142

R

race-based rejection sensitivity, 149–150, 155
race relations assessment, community, 104–105, 133, 164–166